Satisfying Success:
And the Ways to Achieve It

"Tuchy" Palmieri

To my wonderful wife, Susan, who encourages me each and every day to bring happiness and satisfaction to my success and to enjoy the journey.

To our wonderful children–Kathleen, Phil, Amy, John, and Stephen.

To our amazing grandchildren–Sean, Alicia, Heather, Julia, Olivia, C.J., Jack, Will, Tiny II (Julia), Ava, Chris, Sophia, and Adeline–and to all our loved ones.

This book is dedicated to my dad, Filomeno, and my father-in-law, Jurgen; two successful men in their own right. To my uncles Pete, John, Bidz, Peter, Lou, and John, who ventured from their native homeland to find success in the USA. And to all the good women behind them who were keys to their success.

FAMOUS PEOPLE ON SUCCESS (AND SOME NOT SO FAMOUS)

1) *"Try not to be a man of success, but rather to be a man of value." –Albert Einstein*

Suggested Affirmation: "I am a man/woman of value, and living by my values is success."

Suggested Inquiry: Can one be successful if what one truly values is compromised?

Suggested Action: List the values you will live by in order to consider yourself successful.

2) *"Good thoughts and good action lead to good results; bad thoughts and bad action can only lead to bad results." –Og Mandino*

Suggested Affirmation: "I have good thoughts and I follow them up with good action."

Suggested Inquiry: Inquire into the statement that good thoughts are positive, bad thoughts negative, good action springs from positive thoughts and bad action springs from negative thoughts.

Suggested Action: Catch yourself when a negative thought crosses your mind, and cancel it out by purposely replacing it with a positive statement.

FAMOUS PEOPLE ON SUCCESS (AND SOME NOT SO FAMOUS)

" 'Impossible' is just a big word thrown around by small men who find it easier to live in the world they've been given than to explore the power they have to change it. 'Impossible' is not a fact. It's an opinion. 'Impossible' is not a declaration. It's a dare. 'Impossible' is potential. 'Impossible' is temporary. 'Impossible' is nothing."

My affirmations:

_____
_____
_____
_____

What I am inquiring into:

_____
_____
_____
_____

My planned actions:

_____
_____
_____
_____

FAMOUS PEOPLE ON SUCCESS (AND SOME NOT SO FAMOUS)—CONTINUED

3) *"You will be as small as your controlling desire, and as great as your dominate aspiration." –Emerson*

Suggested Affirmation: "I aspire to be free from controlling desires."

Suggested Inquiry: Inquire into the statement that aspirations free one and desires control us.

Suggested Action: Write down what you aspire to.

4) *"You need motivation, and persistence too." –Leon Uris*

Suggested affirmation: "I succeed because I am motivated and I am persistent."

Suggested Inquiry: Inquire into the statement that motivation without persistence has one stop short of success.

Suggested Action: Restart a project or activity in which you were motivated but lacked persistence to bring you one step closer to success.

FAMOUS PEOPLE ON SUCCESS (AND SOME NOT SO FAMOUS)

"I have learned that success is to be measured not so much by the position that one has reached in life as by the obstacles which he has had to overcome while trying to succeed."

—Booker T. Washington

My affirmations:

_____

_____

_____

_____

What I am inquiring into:

_____

_____

_____

_____

My planned actions:

_____

_____

_____

_____

FAMOUS PEOPLE ON SUCCESS (AND SOME NOT SO FAMOUS)—CONTINUED

5)   *"A room without books is like a body without a soul." –Cicero*

Suggested Affirmation: "Books are one of my windows to the world."

Suggested Inquiry: What would the world look like if books were not invented?

Suggested Action: Read a book on a subject you know little or nothing about.

6)   *"Happiness is when what you think, what you say, and what you do are in harmony." –Gandhi*

Suggested Affirmation: "I think happy thoughts, I speak with appreciation, and I live my life as a gift."

Suggested Inquiry: Inquire into the statement that happiness is a choice.

Suggested Action: Think happy thoughts, speak positively, and enjoy the day.

FAMOUS PEOPLE ON SUCCESS (AND SOME NOT SO FAMOUS)

"I find in life that most affairs that require serious handling are distasteful. For this reason, I have always believed that the successful man has the hardest battle with himself rather than with the other fellow. To bring one's self to a frame of mind and to the proper energy to accomplish things that require plain hard work continuously is the one big battle that everyone has. When this battle is won for all time, then everything is easy."

—Thomas Buckner

My affirmations:

_____

_____

_____

What I am inquiring into:

_____

_____

_____

My planned actions:

_____

_____

_____

FAMOUS PEOPLE ON SUCCESS (AND SOME NOT SO FAMOUS)—CONTINUED

7) *"Motivation will almost always beat mere talent." –Norman R. Augustine*

Suggested Affirmation: "I may not be the most talented but I am the most motivated."

Suggested Inquiry: Does motivation beat out talent in many cases?

Suggested Action: Get motivated about something and pursue it.

8) *"Unless a man undertakes more than he possibly can do, he will never do all that he can." –Henry Drummond*

Suggested Affirmation: "'Impossible' is a word found only in the dictionary of fools."

Suggested Inquiry: Does not knowing one's limit help or hinder him?

Suggested Action: Take something in your life where you stopped and go beyond it.

FAMOUS PEOPLE ON SUCCESS (AND SOME NOT SO FAMOUS)

"Defeat may test you; it need not stop you. If at first you don't succeed, try another way. For every obstacle there is a solution. Nothing in the world can take the place of persistence. The greatest mistake is giving up."

–Unknown

My affirmations:

_____

_____

_____

_____

What I am inquiring into:

_____

_____

_____

_____

My planned actions:

_____

_____

_____

_____

FAMOUS PEOPLE ON SUCCESS (AND SOME NOT SO FAMOUS)—CONTINUED

9) *"They may forget what you said, but they will never forget how you make them feel." –Carol Buchner*

Suggested Affirmation: "I live my life with the motto, 'live and let live is good, but live and help live is better.'"

Suggested Inquiry: How must you be to have people feel good when they encounter you?

Suggested Action: Make someone feel good today.

10) *"Success isn't permanent and failure isn't fatal." –Dick Butkus*

Suggested Affirmation: "I am grateful for my successes and I believe the only time we fail is when we stop trying."

Suggested Inquiry: What are the times in your life when you pushed through failure to achieve success?

Suggested Action: Restart something in your life which you gave up on (Guinness record).

FAMOUS PEOPLE ON SUCCESS (AND SOME NOT SO FAMOUS)

"They say time is the best medicine. When you've been through what I have and still keep going through it day after day, you know time isn't all you need. You need God, a few good friends, and a damn break. But time will work for now. Take things step by step. One thing at a time."

–Emmaleigh

My affirmations:

_____

_____

_____

_____

What I am inquiring into:

_____

_____

_____

_____

My planned actions:

_____

_____

_____

_____

FAMOUS PEOPLE ON SUCCESS (AND SOME NOT SO FAMOUS)—CONTINUED

11) *"Motivation will almost always beat mere talent." –Norman R. Augustine*

Suggested Affirmation: "I have a talent for motivation."

Suggested Inquiry: Can anything beat the human soul on fire?

Suggested Action: Use motivation to act and use action to feed more motivation.

12) *"Greatness lies not in being strong, but in the right use of strength." –Henry Ward Beecher*

Suggested Affirmation: "I use my strength wisely and keep my weakness to myself."

Suggested Inquiry: Can wise action create strength from weakness? Look into an area of your life where you can use wisdom to increase your strength.

Suggested Action: Do something great and acknowledge it.

FAMOUS PEOPLE ON SUCCESS (AND SOME NOT SO FAMOUS)

"I don't divide the world into the weak and the strong; or the successes and the failures; those who make it or those who don't. I divide the world into learners and non-learners."

—Unknown

My affirmations:

_____

_____

_____

_____

What I am inquiring into:

_____

_____

_____

_____

My planned actions:

_____

_____

_____

_____

FAMOUS PEOPLE ON SUCCESS (AND SOME NOT SO FAMOUS)—CONTINUED

13) *"A mind troubled by doubt cannot focus on the course to victory." –Arthur Golden*

Suggested Affirmation: "I am a warrior, and a warrior knows that doubt kills."

Suggested Inquiry: When is it appropriate to doubt, and when is it inappropriate?

Suggested Action: Visualize succeeding at an area in which you have some doubt.

14) *"Nothing will ever be attempted if all possible objections must first be overcome." –Samuel Johnson*

Suggested Affirmation: "I take reasonable action and do not allow the need for all the answers to stop me from moving forward."

Suggested Inquiry: Are objections raised when attempting anything new?

Suggested Action: Overcome objections when your heart says yes.

FAMOUS PEOPLE ON SUCCESS (AND SOME NOT SO FAMOUS)

"Behind me is infinite power,
Before me is endless possibility,
Around me is boundless opportunity.
Why should I fear?"

My affirmations:

_____
_____
_____
_____

What I am inquiring into:

_____
_____
_____
_____

My planned actions:

_____
_____
_____
_____
_____

FAMOUS PEOPLE ON SUCCESS (AND SOME NOT SO FAMOUS)—CONTINUED

15) "Do what you can, with what you have, where you are."
  –Theodore Roosevelt

Suggested Affirmation: "I do what I can with what I have."

Suggested Inquiry: How do I know I am doing what I can with what I have?

Suggested Action: Do a little more in any area in which you are not sure if you did all you could.

16) "Prosperity doth best discover vice, but adversity doth best discover virtue." –Francis Bacon

Suggested Affirmation: "I use adversity as a stepping stone and I use money for worthwhile purposes."

Suggested Inquiry: How can one use money for virtuous ends and adversity to turn one to vice?

Suggested Action: Do something virtuous with money, and write down what you found when faced with a memorable adversity.

FAMOUS PEOPLE ON SUCCESS (AND SOME NOT SO FAMOUS)

"In the end, it's extra effort that separates a winner from second place. But winning takes a lot more than that, too. It starts with complete command of the fundamentals. Then it takes desire, determination, discipline, and self-sacrifice. And finally, it takes a great deal of love, fairness, and respect for your fellow man. Put all these together, and even if you don't win, how can you lose?"

—Unknown

My affirmations:

_____
_____
_____
_____

What I am inquiring into:

_____
_____
_____
_____

My planned actions:

_____
_____
_____

FAMOUS PEOPLE ON SUCCESS (AND SOME NOT SO FAMOUS)—CONTINUED

17) *"The world can only be grasped by action, not by contemplation. The hand is the cutting edge of the mind."* *–Jacob Bronowski*

Suggested Affirmation: "I take action as soon as practical."

Suggested Inquiry: Trusting you initial gut feeling is often your best approach.

Suggested Action: When your next action is required, go with your first gut feeling.

18) *"It is time for us to stand and cheer for the doer, the achiever, the one who recognizes the challenge and does something about it."* *–Vince Lombardi*

Suggested Affirmation: "I stand and cheer for doers, including myself."

Suggested Inquiry: Does standing and cheering make a significant difference?

Suggested Action: First, cheer a doer; second, be a doer; and then cheer yourself.

FAMOUS PEOPLE ON SUCCESS (AND SOME NOT SO FAMOUS)

"A true champion is someone who wants to make a difference, who never gives up, and who gives everything she has no matter what the circumstances are. A true champion works hard and never loses sight of her dreams."

–Unknown

My affirmations:

_____
_____
_____
_____

What I am inquiring into:

_____
_____
_____
_____

My planned actions:

_____
_____
_____
_____

FAMOUS PEOPLE ON SUCCESS (AND SOME NOT SO FAMOUS)—CONTINUED

19) "One never notices what has been done; one can only see what remains to be done." –Marie Curie

Suggested Affirmation: "I take note of what has been done and I look forward to what is left to do."

Suggested Inquiry: Looking back makes looking forward easier.

Suggested Action: Each evening, list your accomplishments.

20) "Any coward can fight a battle when he's sure of winning; but give me the man who has the pluck to fight when he's sure of losing." –George Eliot

Suggested Affirmation: I fight one-hundred percent even when the odds are against me.

Suggested Inquiry: Does the uncertainty of winning empower you to action?

Suggested Action: Start something that you had previously given up on.

FAMOUS PEOPLE ON SUCCESS (AND SOME NOT SO FAMOUS)

"It's easy for most people to wait for that one BIG opportunity to come by and land right on their front doorstep. But it usually doesn't happen that way. Small opportunities, when pursued, start to grow into bigger opportunities, little by little, until that seemingly one BIG opportunity falls right into your lap. But it didn't just fall out of thin air. It grew when each small opportunity was thoroughly pursued."

–Brian Kim

My affirmations:

_____
_____
_____
_____

What I am inquiring into:

_____
_____
_____
_____

My planned actions:

_____
_____
_____
_____

FAMOUS PEOPLE ON SUCCESS (AND SOME NOT SO FAMOUS)—CONTINUED

21) *"Many of life's failures are people who did not realize how close they were to success when they gave up." –Thomas Edison*

Suggested Affirmation: "Giving up is the ultimate tragedy."

Suggested Inquiry: Does anyone know how close they are?

Suggested Action: Go the extra step, the extra mile, etc.

22) *"A leader is one who knows the way, goes the way, and shows the way." –John C. Maxwell*

Suggested Affirmation: "I am a leader."

Suggested Inquiry: In what areas of your life are you a leader?

Suggested Action: Take the lead in an area of your life in which you have not led.

FAMOUS PEOPLE ON SUCCESS (AND SOME NOT SO FAMOUS)

"Success: To laugh often and much; to win the respect of intelligent people and the affection of children; to earn the appreciation of honest critics and endure the betrayal of false friends; to appreciate beauty; to find the best in others; to leave the world a bit better; whether by a healthy child, a garden patch, or a redeemed social condition; to know even one life has breathed easier because you have lived. This is to have succeeded!"

–Ralph Waldo Emerson

My affirmations:

_____

_____

_____

_____

What I am inquiring into:

_____

_____

_____

_____

My planned actions:

_____

_____

_____

_____

FAMOUS PEOPLE ON SUCCESS (AND SOME NOT SO FAMOUS)—CONTINUED

23) *"The art of being wise is knowing what to overlook." –William James*

Suggested Affirmation: "I overlook small, unimportant things in favor of important things."

Suggested Inquiry: What can you overlook today that will allow positive events to occur?

Suggested Action: Let go of something that is holding you back.

24) *"Obstacles are those frightful things you see when you take your eyes off your goal." –Henry Ford*

Suggested Affirmation: "I keep my eyes on the goal."

Suggested Inquiry: Minding you own business keeps one focused on the goal.

Suggested Action: Write down a major goal for each area of your life.

FAMOUS PEOPLE ON SUCCESS (AND SOME NOT SO FAMOUS)

"I've missed more than 9000 shots in my career. I've lost almost 300 games. Twenty-six times I've been trusted to take the game-winning shot and missed. I've failed over and over and over again in my life. And that is why I succeed."

—*Michael Jordan*

My affirmations:

_____

_____

_____

_____

What I am inquiring into:

_____

_____

_____

_____

My planned actions:

_____

_____

_____

_____

FAMOUS PEOPLE ON SUCCESS (AND SOME NOT SO FAMOUS)—CONTINUED

25) *"After the game, the king and the pawn go into the same box."*
    –Italian proverb

Suggested Affirmation: "Where I am in relation to others is not as significant as how I relate to them."

Suggested Inquiry: No matter where you are on the scale, the way you relate keeps things in balance.

Suggested Action: Get to the level of the people you meet today.

26) *"Character is like a tree and reputation like its shadow. The shadow is what we think of it; the tree is the real thing."*
    –Abraham Lincoln

Suggested Affirmation: "I do not allow my reputation to overshadow my character."

Suggested Inquiry: Character is built; reputation is earned.

Suggested Action: Live up to your values today.

FAMOUS PEOPLE ON SUCCESS (AND SOME NOT SO FAMOUS)

"DON'T TAKE NO FOR AN ANSWER. It's been said that buyers will say no at least five times before they say yes. It takes persistence to go beyond that first no, to hang in there until the deal is closed. Remember that persistence makes up for a lot of deficiencies you may have."

My affirmations:

_____

_____

_____

_____

What I am inquiring into:

_____

_____

_____

_____

My planned actions:

_____

_____

_____

_____

FAMOUS PEOPLE ON SUCCESS (AND SOME NOT SO FAMOUS)—CONTINUED

27) *"What would you attempt to do if you knew you would not fail?" –Robert Schuler*

Suggested Affirmation: "I invest wisely."

Suggested Inquiry: Failure can be viewed as positive.

Suggested Action: Attempt, fail, and attempt again.

28) *"We never know how far-reaching something we may think, say, or do today will affect the lives of millions tomorrow." –B.J. Palmer*

Suggested Affirmation: "What I say today I say with the knowledge that it will impact others tomorrow."

Suggested Inquiry: How can you be today so that your impact tomorrow will be positive?

Suggested Action: Do something purposeful to positively impact others tomorrow.

FAMOUS PEOPLE ON SUCCESS (AND SOME NOT SO FAMOUS)

"DON'T SELL THE STEAK; SELL THE SIZZLE. Selling the sizzle makes it possible for prospects to smell the steak cooking, to hear the fat dripping into the fire, to see the juices running onto the plate and to taste the smoky barbecue flavor–even when there's nothing in front of them except you. You're not just selling the steak, you're selling the pleasure and satisfaction that steak will bring. And it's your spirit and enthusiasm that makes that happen. If you don't believe in what you're selling, how will the customer?"

My affirmations:

_____
_____
_____
_____

What I am inquiring into:

_____
_____
_____
_____

My planned actions:

_____
_____
_____
_____

FAMOUS PEOPLE ON SUCCESS (AND SOME NOT SO FAMOUS)—CONTINUED

29) *"The superior man is modest in his speech, but exceeds in his actions." –Confucius*

Suggested Affirmation: "I am modest in my speech and exceed most in my actions."

Suggested Inquiry: Often we experience action speaking louder than words.

Suggested Action: Do something for someone without saying a word.

30) *"What comes out of you when you are squeezed is what is inside you." –Wayne Dyer*

Suggested Affirmation: "My best comes forth in troubled times."

Suggested Inquiry: Our best comes forth in troubled times.

Suggested Action: Take action slowly in adversity.

FAMOUS PEOPLE ON SUCCESS (AND SOME NOT SO FAMOUS)

"THE HARDER YOU WORK, THE LUCKIER YOU GET. All the high-achievers I know tell me the secret to their success is basic–hard work. It's doing more than is required. It's that extra push that makes the difference, whether it's getting new prospects, serving current customers, or working with vendors. It's always the extra effort you put in that gets you a 'lucky' break."

My affirmations:

_____
_____
_____
_____

What I am inquiring into:

_____
_____
_____
_____

My planned actions:

_____
_____
_____
_____

FAMOUS PEOPLE ON SUCCESS (AND SOME NOT SO FAMOUS)—CONTINUED

31) "Empowerment is all about letting go so that others can get going." –Kenneth Blanchard

Suggested Affirmation: "I empower others by letting go."

Suggested Inquiry: Does letting go free others to get going?

Suggested Action: Let go of something you have been holding on to and watch what happens.

32) "Too many people overvalue what they are not and undervalue what they are." –Malcolm Forbes

Suggested Affirmation: "I value myself highly."

Suggested Inquiry: Accepting who you are not allows you to be who you are.

Suggested Action: Confirm the acceptance of who you are not by speaking it.

FAMOUS PEOPLE ON SUCCESS (AND SOME NOT SO FAMOUS)

"IT'S NOT WHAT YOU KNOW; IT'S WHO YOU KNOW. Never underestimate the power of each person you meet. You may think someone is unimportant–but you never know how much power that person may have. Seemingly inconsequential contacts you make today may be your most important links to tomorrow's sale. Then, of course, comes the second stage: Once a contact has gotten you through a door, it's what you know that's most important."

My affirmations:

_____
_____
_____
_____

What I am inquiring into:

_____
_____
_____
_____

My planned actions:

_____
_____
_____
_____

FAMOUS PEOPLE ON SUCCESS (AND SOME NOT SO FAMOUS)—CONTINUED

33) *"Anger makes you smaller, while forgiveness forces you to grow beyond what you were." –Cherie Carter-Scott*

Suggested Affirmation: "I use forgiveness to help me grow."

Suggested Inquiry: Where in your life or the lives of others have you seen that forgiveness has led to personal growth?

Suggested Action: Forgive someone or some entity today.

34) *"Not every successful man is a good father. But every good father is a successful man." –Robert Duvall*

Suggested Affirmation: "Being a good father is the highest degree of success."

Suggested Inquiry: Is there anything more important than being a good father?

Suggested Action: Acknowledge your children today.

FAMOUS PEOPLE ON SUCCESS (AND SOME NOT SO FAMOUS)

"ACTIONS SPEAK LOUDER THAN WORDS. Anyone can talk a great game. It's what you do after the talk, after the sale has gone through, and after the promises have been made. It's follow-up and follow-through. That's where trust, service, and future business are built."

My affirmations:

_____
_____
_____
_____

What I am inquiring into:

_____
_____
_____
_____

My planned actions:

_____
_____
_____
_____

FAMOUS PEOPLE ON SUCCESS (AND SOME NOT SO FAMOUS)—CONTINUED

35) *"I talk and talk and talk, and I haven't taught people in fifty years what my father taught by example in one week." –Mario Cuomo*

Suggested Affirmation: "I succeed and teach by example."

Suggested Inquiry: Talk is cheaper than action.

Suggested Action: Be a good example today.

36) *"The tragedy in life doesn't lie in not reaching your goal. The tragedy lies in having no goal to reach." –Benjamin Mays*

Suggested Affirmation: "I set goals for all areas of my life."

Suggested Inquiry: For every vision (GOAL) there are many revisions.

Suggested Action: Write down a new goal and revise the old goals.

FAMOUS PEOPLE ON SUCCESS (AND SOME NOT SO FAMOUS)

"HONESTY IS THE BEST POLICY. Customers never want to hear bad news. They don't want to hear that they have to pay extra or that delivery may take longer. But the best salespeople always tell customers the truth to ensure there are no misunderstandings later on. Customers hate bad news, but they hate unpleasant surprises even more. Honesty and integrity should be your calling cards. They'll create a lifetime of relationships."

My affirmations:

_____
_____
_____
_____

What I am inquiring into:

_____
_____
_____
_____

My planned actions:

_____
_____
_____
_____

FAMOUS PEOPLE ON SUCCESS (AND SOME NOT SO FAMOUS)—CONTINUED

37) *"The highest form of success is making the best of oneself."*
   –Og Mandino

Suggested Affirmation: "I am the best me there is."

Suggested Inquiry: Making the best of oneself is the highest form of success.

Suggested Action: Take a course, read a book, listen to a tape on self-improvement.

38) *"Victory belongs to the most persevering." –Napoleon*

Suggested Affirmation: "I am persevering."

Suggested Inquiry: More often than not persevering helps rather than hinders.

Suggested Action: Persevere with something until you see victory.

FAMOUS PEOPLE ON SUCCESS (AND SOME NOT SO FAMOUS)

"The salespeople who achieve the most are those who practice these basic truths. So don't just let sales cliches go in one ear and out the other. Stop, listen, and think about the nugget of truth that a cliche contains–and what that truth can mean to your sales. Success is an event that accomplishes its intended purpose. It is a state of prosperity or fame. Success is an attainment that is successful. Success is the ultimate goal of any endeavor. We always strive to be successful in whatever we do and success is the sole motive of any operation. Success has a very broad meaning and cannot be defined in some particular terms. It is relative and can never be absolute. Success is what motivates people to strive hard to achieve their goals."

My affirmations:

_____

_____

_____

What I am inquiring into:

_____

_____

_____

My planned actions:

_____

_____

_____

FAMOUS PEOPLE ON SUCCESS (AND SOME NOT SO FAMOUS)—CONTINUED

39) *"DEDICATION: The person who makes a success of living is the one who sees his goal steadily and aims for it unswervingly. That is dedication."* –Cecil B. DeMille

Suggested Affirmation: "I am dedicated."

Suggested Inquiry: Dedication is a key ingredient in success.

Suggested action: Review your goals and clarify when needed.

40) *"If you are to be, you must begin by assuming responsibility. You alone are responsible for every moment of your life, for every one of your acts."* –Antoine de Saint-Exupery

Suggested Affirmation: "I accept responsibility when appropriate."

Suggested Inquiry: Are we truly responsible for every moment of our lives?

Suggested Action: Take responsibility in an area of your life where you are not being responsible.

FAMOUS PEOPLE ON SUCCESS (AND SOME NOT SO FAMOUS)

"To have succeeded is to have finished one's business on earth, like the male spider, who is killed by the female the moment he has succeeded in courtship. I like a state of continual becoming, with a goal in front and not behind."

–*George Bernard Shaw, 28 August 1896*

My affirmations:

_____
_____
_____
_____

What I am inquiring into:

_____
_____
_____
_____

My planned actions:

_____
_____
_____
_____

FAMOUS PEOPLE ON SUCCESS (AND SOME NOT SO FAMOUS)—CONTINUED

41) *"To make our way, we must have firm resolve, persistence, tenacity. We must gear ourselves to work hard all the way. We can never let up." –Ralph Bunche*

Suggested Affirmation: "I gear myself to work hard all the way."

Suggested Inquiry: Most failures occur when we let up.

Suggested Action: Be tenacious today.

42) *"I think a hero is an ordinary individual who finds strength to persevere and endure in spite of overwhelming obstacles." –Christopher Reeve*

Suggested Affirmation: "I am a hero."

Suggested Inquiry: Enduring in spite of overwhelming obstacles is the sign of a true hero.

Suggested Action: Do something ordinary that is heroic.

FAMOUS PEOPLE ON SUCCESS (AND SOME NOT SO FAMOUS)

"Secretary of State Colin Powell once said, 'There are no secrets to success. Don't waste time looking for them. Success is the result of perfection, hard work, learning from failure, loyalty to those for whom you work, and persistence.' The same applies to success in selling."

My affirmations:

_____

_____

_____

_____

What I am inquiring into:

_____

_____

_____

_____

My planned actions:

_____

_____

_____

_____

FAMOUS PEOPLE ON SUCCESS (AND SOME NOT SO FAMOUS)—CONTINUED

43) *"The real contest is always between what you've done and what you're capable of doing. You measure yourself against yourself and nobody else." –Geoffrey Gaberino*

Suggested Affirmation: "I know that I am my only competitor."

Suggested Inquiry: Competing with yourself in a nurturing way is your most rewarding way to compete in life.

Suggested Action: Do what you are capable of doing today.

44) *"Success is never final. Failure is never fatal. Courage is what counts." –Sir Winston Churchill*

Suggested Affirmation: "I will be courageous in the pursuit of my goals."

Suggested Inquiry: Do you let fear of failure stop you? Do you let fear of success stop you?

Suggested Action: Feel the fear, acknowledge it, and take action towards the goal you fear anyway.

FAMOUS PEOPLE ON SUCCESS (AND SOME NOT SO FAMOUS)

"PERSISTENCE. Nothing in the world can take the place of persistence. Talent will not; nothing is more common than unsuccessful men with talent. Genius will not; unrewarded genius is almost a proverb. Education will not; the world is full of educated derelicts. Persistence and determination alone are omnipotent."

–Calvin Coolidge

My affirmations:

_____

_____

_____

_____

What I am inquiring into:

_____

_____

_____

_____

My planned actions:

_____

_____

_____

_____

FAMOUS PEOPLE ON SUCCESS (AND SOME NOT SO FAMOUS)—CONTINUED

45) "The difference between a successful person and others is not a lack of strength, not a lack of knowledge, but rather a lack of will." –Vince Lombardi

Suggested Affirmation: "I have the will; God and I have the will."

Suggested Inquiry: Willingness is the key to most of life's pursuits.

Suggested Action: Put a checkmark next to the goals that you have been unwilling to work on. Decide to be willing, and take an action towards their achievement.

46) "Always bear in mind that your own resolution to success is more important than any other one thing." –Abraham Lincoln

Suggested Affirmation: "My resolve is strong and will get me to act."

Suggested Inquiry: New Year's resolutions are broken more often than not. What is missing is one's resolve.

Suggested Action: Rekindle your resolve through action on an unfulfilled goal.

FAMOUS PEOPLE ON SUCCESS (AND SOME NOT SO FAMOUS)

"The road to success is not straight. There is a curve called Failure, a loop called Confusion, speed bumps called Friends, red lights called Enemies, and caution lights called Family. You will have flats called Jobs. But, if you have a spare called Determination, an engine called Perseverance, insurance called Faith, and a driver called Jesus, you will make it to a place called Success."

My affirmations:

_____
_____
_____
_____

What I am inquiring into:

_____
_____
_____
_____

My planned actions:

_____
_____
_____
_____

FAMOUS PEOPLE ON SUCCESS (AND SOME NOT SO FAMOUS)—CONTINUED

47) *"What we have done for ourselves alone dies with us; what we have done for others and the world remains and is immortal."*
   –Albert Pike

Suggested Affirmation: "The best use of my life is to spend it on things that will outlast it."

Suggested Affirmation: "I will spend part of my life teaching my family."

Suggested Inquiry: What can you do for others today?

Suggested Action: Do a good deed for someone.

48) *"The secret of joy in work is contained in one word–excellence. To know how to do something well is to enjoy it."* *–Pearl S. Buck*

Suggested Affirmation: "I am excellent in many areas of my life."

Suggested Inquiry: Excellence is something to pursue.

Suggested Action: Look into the areas of your life that you are good at now, acknowledge them, and continue to pursue excellence.

FAMOUS PEOPLE ON SUCCESS (AND SOME NOT SO FAMOUS)

"Far better it is to dare mighty things, to win glorious triumphs, even though checkered by failure, than to take rank with those poor spirits who neither enjoy much nor suffer much, because they live in the gray twilight that knows not victory nor defeat."

–Theodore Roosevelt

My affirmations:

_____

_____

_____

_____

What I am inquiring into:

_____

_____

_____

_____

My planned actions:

_____

_____

_____

_____

FAMOUS PEOPLE ON SUCCESS (AND SOME NOT SO FAMOUS)—CONTINUED

49) *"Success-Successful: Coming about, taking place, or turning out as hoped for." –Webster's Dictionary*

Suggested Affirmation: "I am successful because I back up hope with action."

Suggested Inquiry: Adding prayer and work to one's hope improves its chance for success one hundredfold.

Suggested Action: List what you are hoping for. Pray if you believe it is worthwhile, then take some action to move it closer to success.

50) *"Success consists of going from failure to failure without loss of enthusiasm." –Winston Churchill*

Suggested Affirmation: "I continue to be enthusiastic in all my endeavors."

Suggested Inquiry: Faith and courage are great companions of enthusiasm.

Suggested Action: Use positive affirmations to bring a new level of enthusiasm.

FAMOUS PEOPLE ON SUCCESS (AND SOME NOT SO FAMOUS)

"GOALS–It is a paradoxical but profoundly true and important principle of life that the most likely way to reach a goal is to be aiming not at that goal itself but at some more ambitious goal beyond it."

–Arnold Toynbee

My affirmations:

_____

_____

_____

_____

What I am inquiring into:

_____

_____

_____

_____

My planned actions:

_____

_____

_____

_____

FAMOUS PEOPLE ON SUCCESS (AND SOME NOT SO FAMOUS)—CONTINUED

51) *"Success isn't permanent and failure isn't fatal." –Dick Butkus*

Suggested Affirmation: "I know that nothing in life is permanent and yet I continue to pursue success."

Suggested Inquiry: True success is more a matter of one's own decision than the world's judgment.

Suggested Action: Acknowledge success; accept it, enjoy it, and move to the next area to be successful at.

52) *"Success is how high you bounce when you hit bottom." –General George Patton*

Suggested Affirmation: I know that once I hit bottom success starts to germinate.

Suggested Inquiry: Hitting your bottom is like depression–it is the first step towards feeling better.

Suggested Action: Get up, make a change, take a step, and pray to bounce

FAMOUS PEOPLE ON SUCCESS (AND SOME NOT SO FAMOUS)

GRATITUDE IS THE HEART'S MEMORY
"Gratitude unlocks the fullness of life. It turns what we have into enough, and more. It turns denial into acceptance, chaos into order, confusion into clarity. It turns problems into gifts, failures into success, the unexpected into perfect timing and mistakes into important events. Gratitude makes sense of our past, brings peace for today, and creates a vision for tomorrow."

My affirmations:

_____
_____
_____
_____

What I am inquiring into:

_____
_____
_____
_____

My planned actions:

_____
_____
_____
_____

FAMOUS PEOPLE ON SUCCESS (AND SOME NOT SO FAMOUS)—CONTINUED

53) *"It is a rough road that leads to the heights of greatness."*
   –Seneca

Suggested Affirmation: "Taking the high road and the rough road may in reality be the smoothest path to greatness."

Suggested Inquiry: The higher the road the greater one's chance for success.

Suggested Action: Start on one goal that is rough for you and discover that it is not as rough as it first appeared.

54) *"When you lose, don't lose the lesson." –Dali Lama the 14th*

Suggested Affirmation: "I take profit for losses by learning the lessons."

Suggested Inquiry: One never loses if one takes profit from it.

Suggested Action: This evening review your actions, see where losses occurred, write down the lesson learned and take the profit to sleep with you.

FAMOUS PEOPLE ON SUCCESS (AND SOME NOT SO FAMOUS)

"No person can arise above his real desire. Desires are of value only when they drive us to action. Will and work must accompany desire. Then high resolve is born. Desire is the design that will spurs us into achievement."

My affirmations:

_____

_____

_____

_____

What I am inquiring into:

_____

_____

_____

_____

My planned actions:

_____

_____

_____

_____

FAMOUS PEOPLE ON SUCCESS (AND SOME NOT SO FAMOUS)—CONTINUED

55) *"The entrepreneur is essentially a visualizer and an actualizer... He can visualize something, and when he visualizes it he sees exactly how to make it happen." –Robert L. Schwartz*

Suggested Affirmation: "I believe what you see in the mind's eye you can achieve."

Suggested Inquiry: Visualizing strengthens resolve and encourages action that leads to actualization.

Suggested Action: At the beginning of the day spend five minutes visualizing the result you want to occur; put yourself in the picture and make it colorful.

56) *"According to aerodynamic laws, the bumblebee cannot fly. Its body weight is not the right proportion to its wingspan. Ignoring these laws, the bee flies anyway." –M. Sainte-Lague*

Suggested Affirmation: "Like the bumblebee and the humming bird I do not allow limits to be placed on me because others have not achieved it before me."

Suggested Inquiry: Not knowing one's limits allows one to go beyond them.

Suggested Action: Stretch a little farther, bend a little bit more, take one more step than you did last time.

FAMOUS PEOPLE ON SUCCESS (AND SOME NOT SO FAMOUS)

"My mother was the most beautiful woman I ever saw. All I am I owe to my mother. I attribute all my success in life to the moral, intellectual, and physical education I received from her."

–George Washington (1732-1799)

My affirmations:

_____
_____
_____
_____

What I am inquiring into:

_____
_____
_____
_____

My planned actions:

_____
_____
_____
_____

FAMOUS PEOPLE ON SUCCESS (AND SOME NOT SO FAMOUS)—CONTINUED

57) *"Life is either a daring adventure or nothing at all."* –Helen Keller

Suggested Affirmation: "My life is a daring adventure."

Suggested Inquiry: What is it like to live all aspects of your life as a daring adventure?

Suggested Action: Take one area of your life in which you are not living full out, and do so for two days.

58) *"You can't build a reputation on what you are going to do."* –Henry Ford

Suggested Affirmation: "I build my reputation on what I am doing."

Suggested Inquiry: Reputations, like money, are earned.

Suggested Action: Speak less; do more.

FAMOUS PEOPLE ON SUCCESS (AND SOME NOT SO FAMOUS)

"Part of the secret of success in life is to eat what you like and let the food fight it out inside."

—*Mark Twain*

My affirmations:

_____

_____

_____

_____

What I am inquiring into:

_____

_____

_____

_____

My planned actions:

_____

_____

_____

_____

FAMOUS PEOPLE ON SUCCESS (AND SOME NOT SO FAMOUS)—CONTINUED

59) *"Hard work spotlights the character of people: some turn up their sleeves, some turn up their noses, and some don't turn up at all." –Sam Ewig*

Suggested Affirmation: "I turn up my sleeves when called for."

Suggested Inquiry: Your character is always revealed by what you do.

Suggested Action: Roll up your sleeves today.

60) *"The art of resting the mind and the power of dismissing from it all care and worry is probably one of the secrets of our great men." –Captain J.A. Hatfield*

Suggested Affirmation: "Resting my mind is as important as resting my body."

Suggested Inquiry: The resting of one's mind is a developed and determined habit.

Suggested Action: Rest your mind today with meditation and music.

FAMOUS PEOPLE ON SUCCESS (AND SOME NOT SO FAMOUS)

"Instead of solid accomplishments, the man pursues pleasures and self-gratification. He will never achieve anything so long as he is surrounded by dissipating temptations."

–I Ching

My affirmations:

_____
_____
_____
_____

What I am inquiring into:

_____
_____
_____
_____

My planned actions:

_____
_____
_____
_____

FAMOUS PEOPLE ON SUCCESS (AND SOME NOT SO FAMOUS)—CONTINUED

61) *"Success will not lower its standard to us. We must raise our standard to success." –Rev. Randall R. McBride, Jr.*

Suggested Affirmation: "I raise my standard to meet success."

Suggested Inquiry: Raising your standard is a great way to keep growing.

Suggested Action: Raise your standard in an area of your life.

62) *"It's never too late to be who you might have been." –George Elliot*

Suggested Affirmation: "Today I am being who I might have been yesterday."

Suggested Inquiry: Who you might have been is a waste of who you are.

Suggested Action: Take action to be who you want to be.

FAMOUS PEOPLE ON SUCCESS (AND SOME NOT SO FAMOUS)

"Success is not measured by what a man accomplishes, but by the opposition he has encountered and the courage with which he has maintained the struggle against overwhelming odds."

–Charles Lindbergh

My affirmations:

_____
_____
_____
_____

What I am inquiring into:

_____
_____
_____
_____

My planned actions:

_____
_____
_____
_____

FAMOUS PEOPLE ON SUCCESS (AND SOME NOT SO FAMOUS)—CONTINUED

63) *"Talk does not cook rice."* –Chinese proverb

Suggested Affirmation: "My actions speak louder than my words."

Suggested Inquiry: When does talk cook rice?

Suggested Action: Cook rice and do your best.

64) *"Rule your mind or it will rule you."* –Horace

Suggested Affirmation: "I rule my mind by comparing it against the norm."

Suggested Inquiry: When do our minds rule us?

Suggested Action: Write down what you are going to do to rule your mind.

65) *"It is when the well is dry that we know the price of water."*
     –Ben Franklin

Suggested Affirmation: "I know the price of water."

Suggested Inquiry: How can one keep all the wells from drying up?

Suggested Action: Look in your life where the well may be going dry, and dig deeper.

FAMOUS PEOPLE ON SUCCESS (AND SOME NOT SO FAMOUS)

"To bring one's self to a frame of mind and to the proper energy to accomplish things that require plain hard work continuously is the one big battle that everyone has. When this battle is won for all time, then everything is easy."

—*Thomas A. Buckner*

My affirmations:

_____
_____
_____
_____

What I am inquiring into:

_____
_____
_____
_____

My planned actions:

_____
_____
_____
_____

FAMOUS PEOPLE ON SUCCESS (AND SOME NOT SO FAMOUS)—CONTINUED

66) "Nobody who ever gave his best regretted it." –George Halas

Suggested Affirmation: "I am always happy when I feel I have given my best."

Suggested Inquiry: Giving your best and losing is far better than winning without giving your best.

Suggested Action: Take an area of your life in which you are not giving it your best.

67) "Attach yourself to your passion, but not to your pain. Adversity is your best friend on the path to success." –Unknown

Suggested Affirmation: "I am passionate about succeeding."

Suggested Inquiry: We can create passion through our speaking.

Suggested Action: Discover your passion, then go towards your passion.

FAMOUS PEOPLE ON SUCCESS (AND SOME NOT SO FAMOUS)

"Always bear in mind that your own resolution to succeed is more important than any one thing."

—Abraham Lincoln (1809-1865)

My affirmations:

_____
_____
_____
_____

What I am inquiring into:

_____
_____
_____
_____

My planned actions:

_____
_____
_____

FAMOUS PEOPLE ON SUCCESS (AND SOME NOT SO FAMOUS)—CONTINUED

68) *"A successful man is one who can lay a firm foundation with the bricks that others throw at him." –Sidney Greenberg*

Suggested Affirmation: "I do not allow the bricks that people throw at me to become stumbling blocks."

Suggested Inquiry: Doing what you believe is right overshadows people's negativity.

Suggested Action: Consider the words of others; if they do not fit then discard them.

69) *"As one person I cannot change the world, but I can change the world of one person." –Paul Shane Spear*

Suggested Affirmation: "I change the world of the people I love."

Suggested Inquiry: Can we change the world one person at a time?

Suggested Action: Do something good to change the world of one stranger.

FAMOUS PEOPLE ON SUCCESS (AND SOME NOT SO FAMOUS)

"If 'A' is success in life, then 'A' equals 'x' plus 'y' plus 'z.' Work is 'x;' 'y' is play; and 'z' is keeping your mouth shut."

–Albert Einstein (1879-1955) <u>Observer,</u> Jan. 15, 1950

My affirmations:

_____
_____
_____
_____

What I am inquiring into:

_____
_____
_____
_____

My planned actions:

_____
_____
_____
_____

FAMOUS PEOPLE ON SUCCESS (AND SOME NOT SO FAMOUS)—CONTINUED

70) *"To achieve the impossible, one must think the absurd; to look where everyone else has looked, but to see what no one else has seen." –Unknown*

Suggested Affirmation: "I achieve the impossible every day."

Suggested Inquiry: One can achieve the impossible by going beyond it.

Suggested Action: Look and see what no one else has seen.

71) *"A man is not finished when he is defeated. He is finished when he quits." –Richard Nixon*

Suggested Affirmation: "I press on to success."

Suggested Inquiry: A man can fail many times but he is not a failure until he gives up.

Suggested Action: After a defeat stop, then take an action to get profit from it.

FAMOUS PEOPLE ON SUCCESS (AND SOME NOT SO FAMOUS)

"Try not to become a man of success but rather to become a man of value."

–Albert Einstein (1879-1955)

My affirmations:

_____

_____

_____

_____

What I am inquiring into:

_____

_____

_____

_____

My planned actions:

_____

_____

_____

_____

FAMOUS PEOPLE ON SUCCESS (AND SOME NOT SO FAMOUS)—CONTINUED

72) *"Avoid having your ego so close to your position that when your position falls, your ego goes with it." –Colin Powell*

Suggested Affirmation: "My position is my position; it's not me."

Suggested Inquiry: Separating the person from his actions and opinions is a gift to that person and yourself.

Suggested Action: Take an action based upon its right or wrong rather than by your ego.

73) *"The secret of success is consistency of purpose." –Benjamin Disraeli*

Suggested Affirmation: "I stay on purpose by sticking to my plan."

Suggested Inquiry: Discovering one's purpose helps one stay on the path of success.

Suggested Action: Write down your plans and the actions you will take to achieve those plans.

FAMOUS PEOPLE ON SUCCESS (AND SOME NOT SO FAMOUS)

"A great secret of success is to go through life as a man who never gets used up."

–Albert Schweitzer (1875-1965)

My affirmations:

_____
_____
_____
_____

What I am inquiring into:

_____
_____
_____
_____

My planned actions:

_____
_____
_____
_____

FAMOUS PEOPLE ON SUCCESS (AND SOME NOT SO FAMOUS)—CONTINUED

74) *"The lowest ebb is when the tide turns." –Longfellow*

Suggested Affirmation: "I believe the wheel always turns."

Suggested Inquiry: Life has its ups and downs; its highs and lows.

Suggested Action: Take action on a plan, project, or goal that you had given up on.

75) *"I am more afraid of an army of 100 sheep led by a lion than an army of 100 lions led by a sheep." –Talleyrand*

Suggested Affirmation: "I am a lion."

Suggested Inquiry: History is replete with stories of the lionhearted leading a small band of men against a more powerful enemy and winning.

Suggested Action: Get behind a lion or become one yourself on one or more projects.

FAMOUS PEOPLE ON SUCCESS (AND SOME NOT SO FAMOUS)

"A discovery is said to be an accident meeting a prepared mind."

–*Albert Szent-Gyorgyi (1893-1986)*

My affirmations:

_____
_____
_____
_____

What I am inquiring into:

_____
_____
_____
_____

My planned actions:

_____
_____
_____
_____

FAMOUS PEOPLE ON SUCCESS (AND SOME NOT SO FAMOUS)—CONTINUED

76) *"The mind is like a parachute–it works only when it is open."*
–Unknown

Suggested Affirmation: "I keep an open mind to be more of a man."

Suggested Inquiry: "When one opens his mind he hears and sees better." –CJP

Suggested Action: Notice when you are not being open and make a change to be.

77) *"Without a rich heart, wealth is an ugly beggar."* *–Ralph Waldo Emerson*

Suggested Affirmation: "I use every aspect of my wealth in a heartfelt way."

Suggested Inquiry: Money is but one way to get rich.

Suggested Action: Spread the wealth, the entire wealth, to everyone you meet.

FAMOUS PEOPLE ON SUCCESS (AND SOME NOT SO FAMOUS)

"To follow, without halt, one aim: There's the secret of success."

–Anna Pavlova (1885-1931)

My affirmations:

_____
_____
_____
_____

What I am inquiring into:

_____
_____
_____
_____

My planned actions:

_____
_____
_____
_____

FAMOUS PEOPLE ON SUCCESS (AND SOME NOT SO FAMOUS)—CONTINUED

78) *"I can not do everything, but I can do something. I must not fail to do the something that I can do." –Helen Keller*

Suggested Affirmation: "I accept that I cannot do everything and that I must do something."

Suggested Inquiry: Trying to do everything keeps one from doing something.

Suggested Action: Do that something that you do at your very best.

79) *"The secret of success is to do the common things uncommonly well." –John D. Rockefeller*

Suggested Affirmation: "I do common things uncommonly well."

Suggested Inquiry: Doing things uncommonly well makes one stand out.

Suggested Action: Take one of your goals and add action to create the condition of uncommon wellness.

FAMOUS PEOPLE ON SUCCESS (AND SOME NOT SO FAMOUS)

"If your success is not on your own terms, if it looks good to the world but does not feel good in your heart, it is not success at all."

—Anna Quindlen (1953-)

My affirmations:

_____
_____
_____
_____

What I am inquiring into:

_____
_____
_____
_____

My planned actions:

_____
_____
_____
_____

FAMOUS PEOPLE ON SUCCESS (AND SOME NOT SO FAMOUS)—CONTINUED

80) "Self-trust is the first secret of success." –Ralph Waldo Emerson

Suggested Affirmation: "I trust myself, I trust myself, and I trust myself."

Suggested Inquiry: Doubt kills the warrior.

Suggested Action: Write down for each major goal that you trust that you can achieve it.

81) "The kingdom of heaven is within." –Jesus

Suggested Affirmation: "I have the kingdom of heaven at my hands."

Suggested Inquiry: Peace within creates peace without.

Suggested Action: Be kind to yourself by relaxing, meditating, praying, and serving.

FAMOUS PEOPLE ON SUCCESS (AND SOME NOT SO FAMOUS)

"It is possible to fail in many ways, while to succeed is possible only in one way."

–*Aristotle (384 BC-322 BC), <u>Nichomachean Ethics</u>*

My affirmations:

_____
_____
_____
_____

What I am inquiring into:

_____
_____
_____
_____

My planned actions:

_____
_____
_____
_____

FAMOUS PEOPLE ON SUCCESS (AND SOME NOT SO FAMOUS)—CONTINUED

82) *"Happiness is the meaning and purpose of life." –Aristotle*

Suggested Affirmation: "I am achieving God's purpose by being happy."

Suggested Inquiry: Having happiness as one's purpose may not be one's only purpose but it is a key purpose.

Suggested Action: Do something that makes you happy.

83) *"A happy life is all within yourself–your way of being."*
     –Marcus Aurelius

Suggested Affirmation: "I am happy as I am grateful for life."

Suggested Inquiry: You are as happy as you make up your mind to be.

Suggested Action: Make up your mind to be happy; speak about it; let yourself and the world know; then thank God.

FAMOUS PEOPLE ON SUCCESS (AND SOME NOT SO FAMOUS)

"Of course there is no formula for success except perhaps an unconditional acceptance of life and what it brings."

—*Arthur Rubinstein (1886-1982)*

My affirmations:

_____
_____
_____
_____

What I am inquiring into:

_____
_____
_____
_____

My planned actions:

_____
_____
_____
_____

FAMOUS PEOPLE ON SUCCESS (AND SOME NOT SO FAMOUS)—CONTINUED

84) *"You are as happy as you make up your mind to be." –Lincoln*

Suggested Affirmation: "I am as happy as I make up my mind to be."

Suggested Inquiry: Can happiness be totally generated from within?

Suggested Action: Say things and do things that make you happy.

85) *"Success is going from failure to failure with no loss of enthusiasm." –Winston Churchill*

Suggested Affirmation: "I go from failure to failure with no loss of enthusiasm."

Suggested Inquiry: The path of failure after failure is the very path many a successful person has taken.

Suggested Action: Try one more time after a failure.

FAMOUS PEOPLE ON SUCCESS (AND SOME NOT SO FAMOUS)

"Why be a man when you can be a success?"

–Bertolt Brecht (1898-1956)

My affirmations:

_____
_____
_____
_____

What I am inquiring into:

_____
_____
_____
_____

My planned actions:

_____
_____
_____
_____

FAMOUS PEOPLE ON SUCCESS (AND SOME NOT SO FAMOUS)—CONTINUED

86) *"Success is more dangerous than failure." –Lao-tzu (c. 604 B.C.-c. 531 B.C.)*

Suggested Affirmation: "I use my success to help others be successful."

Suggested Inquiry: Success that is used in an inappropriate way is no success at all.

Suggested Action: Take your successes and help someone succeed.

87) *"An accordionist, it has been said, is the only one who can successfully play both ends against the middle." –Rockefeller/ 16th-century English proverb*

Suggested Affirmation: "My life is about helping both ends play."

Suggested Inquiry: Playing both ends against the middle often gets one caught in between.

Suggested Action: Find a situation in which you see one end playing against another and help them to play with each other.

GOALS

"I don't know the key to success, but the key to failure is trying to please everybody."

–Bill Cosby (1937-)

My affirmations:

_____
_____
_____
_____

What I am inquiring into:

_____
_____
_____
_____

My planned actions:

_____
_____
_____
_____

GOALS

1) *"If you don't know where you are going any road will take you there."*

Suggested Affirmation: "I know where I am going and I look for the road that will help me get there."

Suggested Inquiry: You may be on the right road but you will not know it unless you first know where you are going.

Suggested Action: Stop and look at the important areas of your life, and discover, then write down, where you want to go with each.

2) *"Goals are nothing but road markers in life's journey."*

Suggested Affirmation: "I use goals to keep me on track and keep me moving in the right direction."

Suggested Inquiry: If you do not have goals, what do you use for road markers on your journey?

Suggested Action: Make and write down your goals, then write down your actions needed to move closer to achieving them.

GOALS

"What's money? A man is a success if he gets up in the morning and goes to bed at night and in between does what he wants to do."

–Bob Dylan (1941-)

My affirmations:

_____
_____
_____
_____

What I am inquiring into:

_____
_____
_____
_____

My planned actions:

_____
_____
_____
_____

GOALS—CONTINUED

3) "Goals turn 'want' power into willpower."

Suggested Affirmation: "I write my goals and the actions needed to head toward them."

Suggested Inquiry: A goal without subsequent action is not a goal at all.

Suggested Action: Take action on a goal.

4) "A life without goals is like a body without a soul (heart)."
   –Tuchy

Suggested Affirmation: "I have goals for all important aspects of my life."

Suggested Inquiry: Having goals is man's way of taking responsibility for something.

Suggested Action: Review and revise your goals this week.

GOALS

"The person who makes a success of living is the one who sees his goal steadily and aims for it unswervingly. That is dedication."

–Cecil B. DeMille (1881-1959)

My affirmations:

_____

_____

_____

_____

What I am inquiring into:

_____

_____

_____

_____

My planned actions:

_____

_____

_____

_____

GOALS—CONTINUED

5) *"Writing down your goals and actions is like having a goal post–it lets you see the goal and where you must go."*

Suggested Affirmation: "I use action items as a way to bring me closer to the goal."

Suggested Inquiry: A goal without action is but a want without passion.

Suggested Action: Use writing and action as your guideposts.

6) *"Make your life a super goal."*

Suggested Affirmation: "I make my life a super goal."

Suggested Inquiry: A super goal is a goal in which one is striving to be the best he or she can be as a human being.

Suggested Action: Decide on the best you can be and establish goals for it.

GOALS

"Nothing succeeds like the appearance of success."

–Christopher Lasch

My affirmations:

_____

_____

_____

_____

What I am inquiring into:

_____

_____

_____

_____

My planned actions:

_____

_____

_____

_____

GOALS—CONTINUED

7) *"When working towards goals, remember that pyramids were not built in a day."*

Suggested Affirmation: "As long as I am working my goals by taking action, I am at peace with my progress."

Suggested Inquiry: The greatest use of one's life is to spend it on something that will outlast it.

Suggested Action: Do something today that will make a positive difference in someone's life.

8) *"If I were a bird my goal would be to hatch myself everyday."*

Suggested Affirmation: "Each day is a new opportunity for me to be reborn."

Suggested Inquiry: Shifting one's conversation, thoughts, and action creates an opportunity for new birth.

Suggested Action: Make a positive shift in your thoughts on one aspect of your life.

PRESS ON – PERSISTENCE

"There is only one success–to be able to spend your life in your own way."

–Christopher Morley (1890-1957)

My affirmations:

_____
_____
_____
_____

What I am inquiring into:

_____
_____
_____
_____

My planned actions:

_____
_____
_____
_____

PRESS ON - PERSISTENCE

1)   *"Giving up is the ultimate tragedy."*

Suggested Affirmation: "Giving up is not an option."

Suggested Inquiry: All too often success was just a few steps away from when one stopped.

Suggested Action: Make a commitment to do whatever it takes.

2)   *"The only time you fail is when you stop."*

Suggested Affirmation: "When something is not working, I make an adjustment and try again."

Suggested Inquiry: Is history a good yardstick to measure success or failure?

Suggested Action: Get up one more time.

3)   *"The journey of a thousand miles starts with the first step."*

Suggested Affirmation: "Taking the first step is the most important step in the journey."

Suggested Inquiry: Taking one more step, just one more step, is the mantra of success.

Suggested Action: Put one foot in front of another.

PRESS ON – PERSISTENCE

"The man of virtue makes the difficulty to be overcome his first business, and success only a subsequent consideration."

–Confucius (551 BC-479 BC), <u>The Confucian Analects</u>

My affirmations:

_____

_____

_____

_____

What I am inquiring into:

_____

_____

_____

_____

My planned actions:

_____

_____

_____

_____

PRESS ON – PERSISTENCE—CONTINUED

4)   "Failure is the path of least persistence."

Suggested Affirmation: "I persist until failure retreats."

Suggested Inquiry: Quitting is not an option.

Suggested Action: Persist, persist, persist.

5)   "There is no failure except in no longer trying."

Suggested Affirmation: "I keep trying new ways to achieve my goals until I find a way."

Suggested Inquiry: Often it is wise to stop trying a certain path to success and try a new path.

Suggested Action: Take a goal that is not going in the right direction and change its direction by taking a different action.

6)   "The lowest ebb is when the tide turns." –Longfellow

Suggested Affirmation: "The darkest hour is before dawn."

Suggested Inquiry: The darkest hour is when it is the darkest.

Suggested Action: Work with the tide, not against it.

PRESS ON – PERSISTENCE

"Real success is finding your lifework in the work that you love."

–David McCullough (1933-)

My affirmations:

_____
_____
_____
_____

What I am inquiring into:

_____
_____
_____
_____

My planned actions:

_____
_____
_____
_____

PRESS ON – PERSISTENCE—CONTINUED

7) "The journey of a thousand miles starts with the first step."

Suggested Affirmation: "I start and take action on my goals and projects."

Suggested Inquiry: Beginning now on long-term projects is the key to their realization.

Suggested Action: List all the areas in which action has not begun, and then take a step.

8) "Failure is the path of least persistence."

Suggested Affirmation: "I am a persistent son-of-a-gun."

Suggested Inquiry: Persistence is a quality that can be learned.

Suggested Action: Find a goal or project that is not moving, and take action on that goal or project each day until it is done.

9) "There is no failure except in no longer trying."

Suggested Affirmation: "I do not believe in failure."

Suggested Inquiry: The only time you fail is when you stop trying.

Suggested Action: Restart an idle goal or project by taking action on it.

PRESS ON – PERSISTENCE

"Success in business requires training and discipline and hard work. But if you're not frightened by these things, the opportunities are just as great today as they ever were."

–David Rockefeller (1915-)

My affirmations:

_____
_____
_____
_____

What I am inquiring into:

_____
_____
_____
_____

My planned actions:

_____
_____
_____
_____

PRESS ON – PERSISTENCE—CONTINUED

10) "The lowest ebb is when the tide turns." –Longfellow

Suggested Affirmation: "I know that the wheel always turns and that failure turns into success."

Suggested Inquiry: Just when one is ready to give up, a light shines–all we need do is look for it.

Suggested Action: Take a goal or project in which you have had the smallest amount of success and take another positive action.

11) "No one knows the number of attempts, missteps, and slips one must take before success arrives."

Suggested Affirmation: "I willingly take the steps necessary to succeed."

Suggested Inquiry: Are you willing to continue with little or no progress?

Suggested Action: Take one more step.

PRESS ON – PERSISTENCE

"Aim for success; not perfection. Never give up your right to be wrong, because then you will lose the ability to learn new things and move forward with your life."

–Dr. David M. Burns

My affirmations:

_____
_____
_____
_____

What I am inquiring into:

_____
_____
_____
_____

My planned actions:

_____
_____
_____
_____

PRESS ON – PERSISTENCE—CONTINUED

12) *"Success is fathered by persistence and failure is the orphan of apathy."*

Suggested Affirmation: "I use persistence as the tool that keeps apathy away."

Suggested Inquiry: Restart any area in your life in which you have let apathy stop you.

Suggested Action: Go beyond your normal stopping point.

13) *"Three most important qualities that makes one succeed– action, action, action."*

Suggested Affirmation: "I always take action when it's appropriate."

Suggested Inquiry: Does fear stop you from taking action?

Suggested Action: Write down the areas in your life in which no action has been taken for one month. Choose one action to take, then choose another and another and take one action a day for seven days.

PRESS ON – PERSISTENCE

"We succeed only as we identify in life, or in war, or in anything else, a single overriding objective, and make all other considerations bend to that one objective."

–Dwight D. Eisenhower (1890-1969), Speech;
April 2, 1957

My affirmations:

_____
_____
_____
_____

What I am inquiring into:

_____
_____
_____
_____

My planned actions:

_____
_____
_____
_____

PRESS ON – PERSISTENCE—CONTINUED

14) "Today's success is yesterday's failure that did not give up."

Suggested Affirmation: "I am successful in life because I do not give up."

Suggested Inquiry: Getting unstuck is simple but not easy.

Suggested Action: Write down the different approaches you can take to succeed on a goal, then pick one, and take action.

15) "Any success worthwhile must be pursued and pursued."

Suggested Affirmation: "Many of my greatest satisfactions, and my greatest successes, came from my longest pursuits."

Suggested Inquiry: What makes a goal worth pursuing against all odds?

Suggested Action: List what goals you no longer want to pursue. Commit to not pursuing, and use that energy to pursue other goals by taking additional action on them.

PRESS ON – PERSISTENCE

"Success is counted sweetest by those who ne'er succeed."

–Emily Dickinson (1830-1886)

My affirmations:

_____
_____
_____
_____

What I am inquiring into:

_____
_____
_____
_____

My planned actions:

_____
_____
_____
_____

PRESS ON – PERSISTENCE—CONTINUED

16) "Persistence is the foundation of education."

Suggested Affirmation: "I learn by being persistent."

Suggested Inquiry: Persistence is the most important quality in a young child's learning, such as crawling, walking, and riding a bike.

Suggested Action: Take an area of your life in which you have said you are not good at and use renewed persistence to change that.

17) "Success is getting up just one more time than you fall down."

Suggested Affirmation: "My greatest glory comes not from never failing but in rising every time I fall."

Suggested Inquiry: Getting up one more time is the key to success in many challenges.

Suggested Action: Write down the achievements you made as a child that resulted from getting up just one more time than when you fell.

DREAMS

"Success didn't spoil me; I've always been insufferable."

–Fran Lebowitz (1950-)

My affirmations:

_____

_____

_____

_____

What I am inquiring into:

_____

_____

_____

_____

My planned actions:

_____

_____

_____

_____

DREAMS

1)   "What you can dream you can achieve."

Suggested Affirmation: "I dream and visualize achieving my goal as a way of achieving it."

Suggested Inquiry: Dreaming about what you want helps to make what you want come true.

Suggested Action: For seven days, take a different goal and dream about it and visualize achieving it, then see yourself having achieved it.

2)   "Dream the impossible dream."

Suggested Affirmation: "I freely dream my dream without restriction as to its possibility."

Suggested Inquiry: Dreaming what you want with no restrictions makes the seemingly impossible, possible.

Suggested Action: Take something you believe is impossible, and dream about it each evening for seven days.

DREAMS

"Nothing changes your opinion of a friend so surely as success– yours or his."

—*Franklin P. Jones; <u>Saturday Evening Post</u>, November 29, 1953*

My affirmations:

_____
_____
_____
_____

What I am inquiring into:

_____
_____
_____
_____

My planned actions:

_____
_____
_____

DREAMS—CONTINUED

3) *"If your dreams do not come true, try worrying about what you want, and dreaming about what you do not want."*

Suggested Affirmation: "What I consistently dream about always comes true."

Suggested Inquiry: Worrying is merely negative visualization.

Suggested action: Tonight, dream purposefully.

4) *"Life is a dream for the wise, a game for the fool, a comedy for the rich, and a tragedy for the poor." –Unknown*

Suggested Affirmation: "Life is a dream for me."

Suggested Inquiry: Can we change our lives by the way we think?

Suggested Action: Think of life as a dream.

DREAMS

"I owe my success to having listened respectfully to the very best advice, and then going away and doing the exact opposite."

–G. K. Chesterton (1874-1936)

My affirmations:

_____
_____
_____
_____

What I am inquiring into:

_____
_____
_____
_____

My planned actions:

_____
_____
_____
_____

DREAMS—CONTINUED

5) *"All too often sweet dreams turn into sweat dreams."*

Suggested Affirmation: "I create my opportunities by taking action."

Suggested Inquiry: Opportunities create new opportunities through action. What is your best way to create opportunities?

Suggested Action: Act on an opportunity and have that opportunity create a new opportunity.

6) *"If you can see it in you mind's eye and in your heart, you can see it in the world."*

Suggested Affirmation: "A positive result comes about from my action."

Suggested Inquiry: A small result is but a small step in the right direction.

Suggested Action: Write down small steps that you took today and say, "thank you."

FAILURE/MANIFESTATION

"Nothing fails like success."

–Gerald Nachman

My affirmations:

_____
_____
_____
_____

What I am inquiring into:

_____
_____
_____
_____

My planned actions:

_____
_____
_____
_____

FAILURE/MANIFESTATION

1) *"In everyone's book of life you can find chapters of failure."*

Suggested Affirmation: "I take failures as just chapters when, once read and passed, success begins to arrive."

Suggested Inquiry: How can you use your failures as stepping stones?

Suggested Action: Finish a chapter in which failure occurred by taking action to start another chapter.

2) *"'Failure' is found in the dictionary between 'doubt' and 'fear.'"*

Suggested Affirmation: "I overcome fear and doubt by taking action."

Suggested Inquiry: How does commitment and faith override doubt and fear?

Suggested Action: Feel the fear, have the doubt, and do it anyway.

FAILURE/MANIFESTATION

"To freely bloom: That is my definition of success."

> –Gerry Spence, <u>How to Argue and Win Every Time</u>

My affirmations:

_____

_____

_____

_____

What I am inquiring into:

_____

_____

_____

_____

My planned actions:

_____

_____

_____

_____

FAILURE/MANIFESTATION—CONTINUED

3)   *"Success can be purchased with the profits from past failures."*

Suggested Affirmation: "I purchase success from the earnings of my previous failures."

Suggested Inquiry: What makes failure the single most important ingredient of success?

Suggested Action: Take what you have earned from a previous failure and purchase success.

4)   *"There is no failure except in no longer trying."*

Suggested Affirmation: "I never fail as I always keep trying."

Suggested Inquiry: Is there a time when it is appropriate to stop trying?

Suggested Action: Write down the failures you had that were a result of you stopping to try.

FAILURE/MANIFESTATION

"My mother drew a distinction between achievement and success. She said that achievement is the knowledge that you have studied and worked hard and done the best that is in you. Success is being praised by others, and that's nice, too, but not as important or satisfying. Always aim for achievement and forget about success."

–Helen Hayes (1900-1993)

My affirmations:

_____

_____

_____

_____

What I am inquiring into:

_____

_____

_____

_____

My planned actions:

_____

_____

_____

_____

FAILURE/MANIFESTATION—CONTINUED

5) *"Failures wait for opportunities; successful people create them."*

Suggested Affirmation: "I create opportunities through my speaking and my action."

Suggested Inquiry: If taking action, visualizing, and speaking each contribute to the achievement of a goal, how might doing all three contribute?

Suggested Action: See your goal achieved, speak its achievement, and take a step towards its achievement.

6) *"The successful person is motivated by small results from big efforts and the failure is discouraged by them."*

Suggested Affirmation: "I have a high tolerance for no results."

Suggested Inquiry: In many cases one cannot see results until well after the chain of events necessary to create the results has occurred.

Suggested Action: Take action in the face of no results.

FAILURE/MANIFESTATION

"Men are born to succeed, not fail."

–Henry David Thoreau (1817-1862)

My affirmations:

_____
_____
_____
_____

What I am inquiring into:

_____
_____
_____
_____

My planned actions:

_____
_____
_____
_____

FAILURE/MANIFESTATION—CONTINUED

7) *"The bigger the failures you are willing to accept, the greater the successes you can achieve."*

Suggested Affirmation: "I am willing to risk failure to attempt something important to me."

Suggested Inquiry: The bigger the project, the bigger the failures, so have big failures.

Suggested Action: After a big failure, begin again towards that worthy goal.

8) *"The higher your tolerance for failure, the greater your chances for success."*

Suggested Affirmation: "I have a high tolerance for failure."

Suggested Inquiry: In the face of failure, successful people keep going.

Suggested Action: Go beyond your previous level of tolerance.

FAILURE/MANIFESTATION

"Success usually comes to those who are too busy to be looking for it."

—*Henry David Thoreau (1817-1862)*

My affirmations:

_____

_____

_____

_____

What I am inquiring into:

_____

_____

_____

_____

My planned actions:

_____

_____

_____

_____

FAILURE/MANIFESTATION—CONTINUED

9)   "Most failed attempts bring one closer to achievement."

Suggested Affirmation: "Often what we perceive as failure is but a step on the path of success."

Suggested Inquiry: Looking back can you now see that what you have seen in the past as a failure was actually a necessary step to success?

Suggested Action: Review a past failure and look at it from the perspective of just another necessary step.

10)   "Use the law of averages and the odds to achieve success."

Suggested Affirmation: "I use the law of averages and bet with the odds to achieve success."

Suggested Inquiry: One's chances of success increase each time an attempt is made.

Suggested Action: Improve your odds of success on a project by taking an action towards it.

FAILURE/MANIFESTATION

"Each success only buys an admission ticket to a more difficult problem."

–Henry Kissinger (1923-); <u>Wilson Library Bulletin,</u> March 1979

My affirmations:

_____
_____
_____
_____

What I am inquiring into:

_____
_____
_____
_____

My planned actions:

_____
_____
_____
_____

FAILURE/MANIFESTATION—CONTINUED

11) "If you want to succeed you must learn to live with failure."

Suggested Affirmation: "I not only live with failure, but I know failure is actually my friend that stays with me until no longer needed."

Suggested Inquiry: Can failure be one's friend on the path to success?

Suggested Action: Look at a recent failure and list the different actions one can make towards its achievement.

12) "More wisdom is gained from failure than from success."

Suggested Affirmation: "I gain wisdom from my failures by taking profit from them."

Suggested Inquiry: One can always take profit from failure.

Suggested Action: Find the profit in your last failure.

FAILURE/MANIFESTATION

"I can't give you a sure-fire formula for success, but I can give you a formula for failure: try to please everybody all the time."

—*Herbert Bayard Swope (1882-1958)*

My affirmations:

_____
_____
_____
_____

What I am inquiring into:

_____
_____
_____
_____

My planned actions:

_____
_____
_____
_____

FAILURE/MANIFESTATION—CONTINUED

13) *"At times the price of failure is higher than the price of success." –Tuchy*

Suggested Affirmation: "When the price of failure exceeds the price of success, I will succeed."

Suggested Inquiry: In many cases the cost of failure can be eliminated by spending more on action.

Suggested Action: Take action when appropriate after weighing the cost.

14) *"In most cases the more significant the success, the more failures one must endure to achieve it."*

Suggested Affirmation: "I am prepared and willing to keep working until I succeed."

Suggested Inquiry: Often the most rewarding achievements take a lifetime.

Suggested Action: Work on the goals and projects that are worthy of your attention and effort.

FAILURE/MANIFESTATION

"The toughest thing about success is that you've got to keep on being a success. Talent is only a starting point in this business. You've got to keep on working that talent. Someday I'll reach for it and it won't be there."

–Irving Berlin

My affirmations:

_____
_____
_____
_____

What I am inquiring into:

_____
_____
_____
_____

My planned actions:

_____
_____
_____
_____
_____

FAILURE/MANIFESTATION—CONTINUED

15) "Success isn't permanent and failure isn't fatal." –Dick Butkus

Suggested Affirmation: "I continue with my success as I continue to work at succeeding."

Suggested Inquiry: Some success and achievements are time-bound.

Suggested Action: Acknowledge any previous success that you have had and can no longer achieve by celebrating it, accepting it, and being grateful for it.

16) "Succeeding at suicide is one's greatest failure, and failing at suicide can be a successful act."

Suggested Affirmation: "The darkest hour comes before dawn, and I will pass through my darkest hour and become stronger for it."

Suggested Inquiry: Reaching out for help is what we are called to do by God.

Suggested Action: Reach out for help during the dark times and they will bring you light.

FAILURE/MANIFESTATION

"The secret of success is sincerity. Once you can fake that you've got it made."

–Jean Giraudoux (1882-1944)

My affirmations:

_____
_____
_____
_____

What I am inquiring into:

_____
_____
_____
_____

My planned actions:

_____
_____
_____
_____

FAILURE/MANIFESTATION—CONTINUED

17) "Failures are like hot potatoes–hard to handle."

Suggested Affirmation: "I am a cool cucumber."

Suggested Inquiry: Calming down in many cases is the most important ingredient needed to succeed.

Suggested Action: When failure and frustration stare you in the face, breathe and relax, then make another attempt.

18) "Failures are but fouls in the game of life."

Suggested Affirmation: "I may do foolish things at times but I am no fool."

Suggested Inquiry: Often it is our foolishness that leads us to failure.

Suggested Action: Discover a goal or project in which you have been foolish, decide on an appropriate action, then take it to see if your results change.

FAILURE/MANIFESTATION

"If you wish success in life, make perseverance your bosom friend, experience your wise counselor, caution your elder brother and hope your guardian genius."

–Joseph Addison (1672-1719)

My affirmations:

_____

_____

_____

_____

What I am inquiring into:

_____

_____

_____

_____

My planned actions:

_____

_____

_____

_____

FAILURE/MANIFESTATION—CONTINUED

19) "The most crippling diseases that lead to failure... excuses."

Suggested Affirmation: "We have reasons and we have results, and I have results."

Suggested Inquiry: We are either busy giving reasons or busy achieving results.

Suggested Action: The next time you catch yourself making excuses, stop and take action toward your project or goal.

20) "The single most common element in failure is inaction."

Suggested Affirmation: "I take action when appropriate."

Suggested Inquiry: Inaction more often than not brings failure closer rather than success.

Suggested action: TAKE ACTION.

FAILURE/MANIFESTATION

"There's no secret about success. Did you ever know a successful man who didn't tell you about it?"

—Kin Hubbard (1868-1930)

My affirmations:

_____
_____
_____
_____

What I am inquiring into:

_____
_____
_____
_____

My planned actions:

_____
_____
_____
_____

FAILURE/MANIFESTATION—CONTINUED

21) *"Today's success often becomes tomorrow's failure and today's failure often becomes tomorrow's success."*

Suggested Affirmation: "I keep going and I roll with the punches."

Suggested Inquiry: Failure and success are for everyone.

Suggested Action: Take action as if you were to succeed.

22) *"It is through failure that we find the path of success."*

Suggested Affirmation: "I see failure as part of success."

Suggested Inquiry: Seeing failure as just a step on the path to success relieves considerable anxiety.

Suggested Action: Write down the failures you have had on your most difficult goal or project.

FAILURE/MANIFESTATION

"A successful individual typically sets his next goal somewhat, but not too much, above his last achievement. In this way he steadily raises his level of aspiration."

–Kurt Lewin (1890-1947)

My affirmations:

_____
_____
_____
_____

What I am inquiring into:

_____
_____
_____
_____

My planned actions:

_____
_____
_____
_____

FAILURE/MANIFESTATION—CONTINUED

23) *"Some of the most grateful people are those who failed at attempting suicide."*

Suggested Affirmation: "I pray for all who are struggling with life and want to leave it."

Suggested Inquiry: The root cause of many suicides is low self-esteem.

Suggested Action: Reach out to someone who had attempted suicide.

24) *"Being busy doing what you are not doing is the surest way to failure."*

Suggested Affirmation: "I focus on what I am doing at the moment."

Suggested Inquiry: Are we normally busy doing what we are not doing?

Suggested Action: Be attentive to your task and write down the moments when you do what you are not doing.

TRUISMS

"All you need in this life is ignorance and confidence; then success is sure."

–Mark Twain (1835-1910); Letter to Mrs. Foote,
Dec. 2, 1887

My affirmations:

_____
_____
_____
_____

What I am inquiring into:

_____
_____
_____
_____

My planned actions:

_____
_____
_____
_____

TRUISMS

1) *"How a man thinks he is in his heart, so he is."*

Suggested Affirmation: "I think good thoughts, and when I do not, I reject them and think a positive thought around the situation."

Suggested Inquiry: Can we have a change of heart by changing our thoughts?

Suggested Action: Take a heartache and think about it differently.

2) *"Thinking your way to success is possible when it is followed up with action that is consistent with it."*

Suggested Affirmation: "I affirm success and I follow that up with action."

Suggested Inquiry: Can we think our way to success without taking action?

Suggested Action: Speak and act affirmingly on a goal.

TRUISMS

"People fail forward to success."

–Mary Kay Ash

My affirmations:

_____
_____
_____
_____

What I am inquiring into:

_____
_____
_____
_____

My planned actions:

_____
_____
_____
_____

TRUISMS—CONTINUED

3) "We learn more from failure than we learn from success. "

Suggested Affirmation: "I learn what not to do every time I fail and that helps me learn what to do."

Suggested Inquiry: Doing what does not work gets one closer to doing what works.

Suggested Action: Each time you fail at something, take the time to write down the lesson learned to take profit from the loss.

4) "Failure is your teacher. "

Suggested Affirmation: "Failure is indeed my teacher."

Suggested Inquiry: Making a friend of failure and having it be one's teacher is a powerful position.

Suggested Action: Thank your teachers at the end of the day.

5) "Believe you can succeed and you can, "

Suggested Affirmation: "I believe I can succeed and I will."

Suggested Inquiry: If you say you can and if you say you cannot, you are right.

Suggested Action: Say you can anew.

CARL "TUCHY" PALMIERI

TRUISMS

"Whenever I hear, 'It can't be done,' I know I'm close to success."

–Michael Flatley, (Lord of the Dance); quoted by Eric Celeste

My affirmations:

_____
_____
_____
_____

What I am inquiring into:

_____
_____
_____
_____

My planned actions:

_____
_____
_____
_____

TRUISMS—CONTINUED

6)   "To succeed in any journey one must be willing to start."

Suggested Affirmation: "I am a quick starter."

Suggested Inquiry: Taking action is one of the common elements necessary for success.

Suggested Action: Take any goal or project in which no action has occurred and start on it.

7)   "Letting go can be as important as hanging on."

Suggested Affirmation: "I let go when it is appropriate to let go."

Suggested Inquiry: The metaphor of the bird letting go of the worm allows one the freedom to let go without giving up on a goal.

Suggested Action: Let go and let God with one difficult aspect of your life.

TRUISMS

"You always pass failure on the way to success."

–Mickey Rooney (1920-)

My affirmations:

_____
_____
_____
_____

What I am inquiring into:

_____
_____
_____
_____

My planned actions:

_____
_____
_____
_____

TRUISMS—CONTINUED

8)   *"Four things do not return–the spoken word, a sped arrow, the past life, and a lost opportunity."*

Suggested Affirmation: "I understand that certain things in life are not returnable."

Suggested Inquiry: Choosing wisely how one lets go of what does not return is one of life's biggest challenges.

Suggested Action: Write down what you plan to do with your spoken words and the opportunities before you before taking action.

9)   *"Good thoughts and good action lead to good results; bad thoughts and bad action can only lead to bad results."* –Og Mandino

Suggested Affirmation: "I have good thoughts and take good action."

Suggested Inquiry: Replacing bad thoughts with good thoughts is the eraser of the mind.

Suggested Action: Whenever you become aware of a negative though, consciously replace it with the opposite positive thought.

TRUISMS

"Success isn't permanent, and failure isn't fatal."

–Mike Ditka (1939-)

My affirmations:

_____
_____
_____
_____

What I am inquiring into:

_____
_____
_____
_____

My planned actions:

_____
_____
_____
_____

TRUISMS—CONTINUED

10) "Climbing success mountain is seldom done alone."

Suggested Affirmation: "I welcome people's help on my journey up success mountain."

Suggested Inquiry: Eventually we fall off success mountain if we climb it alone.

Suggested Action: Give someone in your life an opportunity to help you.

11) "When it comes to success we have reasons or results."

Suggested Affirmation: "I do not let reasons stop me from succeeding."

Suggested Inquiry: Often reasons are but disguised excuses.

Suggested Action: Have your reasons and do it anyway.

TRUISMS

"Formulate and stamp indelibly on your mind a mental picture of yourself as succeeding. Hold this picture tenaciously. Never permit it to fade. Your mind will seek to develop the picture. Do not build up obstacles in your imagination."

–Norman Vincent Peale (1898-1993)

My affirmations:

_____
_____
_____
_____

What I am inquiring into:

_____
_____
_____
_____

My planned actions:

_____
_____
_____
_____

TRUISMS—CONTINUED

12) "The oak sleeps in the acorn."

Suggested Affirmation: "I know that just because I cannot see my end result, I know it is there."

Suggested Inquiry: Looking at goals and projects from the perspective of the oak sleeping in the acorn allows one to forge ahead with little or no visible results.

Suggested Action: Affirm that steps you take today all bring results, even if they are not noticeable.

13) "The un-driven do not get there."

Suggested Affirmation: "I am a person with drive."

Suggested Inquiry: Letting things happen is one way to go through life, but making things happen is living life.

Suggested Action: Take one more step today.

TRUISMS

"Success is not the result of spontaneous combustion. You must set yourself on fire."

—Reggie Leach

My affirmations:

_____
_____
_____
_____

What I am inquiring into:

_____
_____
_____
_____

My planned actions:

_____
_____
_____
_____

TRUISMS—CONTINUED

14) "Never let yesterday use up today."

Suggested Affirmation: "I let go of yesterday as being complete."

Suggested Inquiry: Letting go of yesterday is one of the most powerful uses of the principle of letting go.

Suggested Action: Look into your life in which an event of the past has you reliving it over and over, and declare it complete.

15) "The weeds of discontent kill the fruit of wealth."

Suggested Affirmation: "I do not allow discontent to replace contentment."

Suggested Inquiry: Wanting more and better often takes away the enjoyment of what one has.

Suggested Action: Thank God for the abundance in your life.

TRUISMS

"A minute's success pays the failure of years."

–Robert Browning (1812-1889)

My affirmations:

_____

_____

_____

_____

What I am inquiring into:

_____

_____

_____

_____

My planned actions:

_____

_____

_____

_____

TRUISMS—CONTINUED

16) "The weeds of discontent kill the seeds of wealth."

Suggested Affirmation: "I do not allow the weeds of negative thinking to kill the seeds of positive thought."

Suggested Inquiry: We may not be able to choose all our thoughts but we can always choose to replace negative thoughts with positive thoughts.

Suggested Action: At day's end, mentally review it and weed out any negative thoughts that remain by replacing them with positive thoughts.

17) "The flower that yields honey for the bee also provides poison for the spider."

Suggested Affirmation: "Before I take action I project the anticipated results. If the projection is good, then I continue."

Suggested Inquiry: Projection is a tool that, when used positively, can yield more effective action.

Suggested Action: When faced with alternative actions, use projection to help determine the appropriate one.

TRUISMS

"Success is the ability to go from one failure to another with no loss of enthusiasm."

–Sir Winston Churchill (1874-1965)

My affirmations:

_____

_____

_____

_____

What I am inquiring into:

_____

_____

_____

_____

My planned actions:

_____

_____

_____

_____

TRUISMS—CONTINUED

18) *"If you say you can, you ARE RIGHT; if you say you cannot, you ARE RIGHT."*

Suggested Affirmation: "I know how powerful my speaking is and I am careful to speak powerfully and positively to achieve success."

Suggested Inquiry: Knowing that you are right with your words regardless allows one to use them powerfully.

Suggested Action: Make something right with your words.

19) *"Succeeding at bad things is far worse than failing at good things."*

Suggested Affirmation: "Before I commit to a goal, I look at its impact. If it has an overall negative impact, I revise the goal before committing to it."

Suggested Inquiry: It is often easier to succeed at negative things than it is for the positive things.

Suggested Action: Review your goals and look at them from the viewpoint of positive or negative impact, and eliminate or revise any that will result in a negative outcome.

TRUISMS

"Many of life's failures are people who did not realize how close they were to success when they gave up."

–Thomas A. Edison (1847-1931)

My affirmations:

_____
_____
_____
_____

What I am inquiring into:

_____
_____
_____
_____

My planned actions:

_____
_____
_____
_____

TRUISMS—CONTINUED

20) "When all else fails, follow the success of others."

Suggested Affirmation: "I learn from others."

Suggested Inquiry: Can one learn from watching the success and failure of others?

Suggested Action: Find the person who has what you want in a particular area, ask that person what they did to achieve it, and do the same.

21) "Every great accomplishment owes its greatness to the failures along the way."

Suggested Affirmation: "Failed attempts are also my teachers."

Suggested Inquiry: Observing both success and failure gives one a clearer picture of what must be done to succeed.

Suggested Action: Take a failed attempt and write down what specifically did not work.

TRUISMS

"Under-promise; over-deliver."

—Tom Peters, in *The Chicago Tribune*

My affirmations:

_____
_____
_____
_____

What I am inquiring into:

_____
_____
_____
_____

My planned actions:

_____
_____
_____
_____

TRUISMS—CONTINUED

22) "Great accomplishments are achieved through failure."

Suggested Affirmation: "Each failure brings me closer to my success."

Suggested Inquiry: Knowing what does not work is a valid way to discover what does work.

Suggested Action: Find the successful part of each failure and build on it.

23) "The wise man uses his failures as stepping stones; the fool has them be stumbling blocks."

Suggested Affirmation: "With each attempt I discover what worked and I keep that for my next attempt."

Suggested Inquiry: Taking the good from the bad is a valid path to success.

Suggested Action: Acknowledge every attempt that brings you closer to success.

TRUISMS

"I know of only one bird–the parrot–that talks, and it can't fly very high."

–Wilbur Wright (1867-1912), declining to make a speech in 1908

My affirmations:

_____

_____

_____

_____

What I am inquiring into:

_____

_____

_____

_____

My planned actions:

_____

_____

_____

_____

TRUISMS—CONTINUED

24) "The difference between building blocks and stumbling blocks is that building blocks sit on top of each other."

Suggested Affirmation: "I build upon each attempt by repeating the part that worked."

Suggested Inquiry: Keeping the working facets of failed attempts is often the surest way to success.

Suggested Action: Review a failed attempt in your mind until you discover and commit to using the portions that worked to build on.

25) "The morning has more wisdom than the evening."

Suggested Affirmation: "I take action towards my goals when I am alert and the day is fresh."

Suggested Inquiry: Finding when one is most productive is an important key to one's success.

Suggested Action: Make attempts during specific times of the day to establish your peak performance time.

TRUISMS

"Eighty percent of success is showing up."

—*Woody Allen (1935-)*

My affirmations:

_____
_____
_____
_____

What I am inquiring into:

_____
_____
_____
_____

My planned actions:

_____
_____
_____
_____
_____

TRUISMS—CONTINUED

26) *"Success is a journey and the missteps are but part of the journey."*

Suggested Affirmation: "Going in the right direction does not mean that every step is identical to the last and that some steps are but corrections of a previous step or series of steps."

Suggested Inquiry: A step in the right direction need not be a perfect step to get one closer to the goal as a subsequent imperfect step brings perfection.

Suggested Action: Take corrective steps as soon as you determine one is needed.

27) *"Be grateful for your failures, for they make success possible."*

Suggested Affirmation: "I am grateful that I made an attempt and look forward to attempting again."

Suggested Inquiry: Looking at each attempt in a positive way helps one get closer to the successful attempt.

Suggested Action: Acknowledge every attempt and affirm that you are a step closer to success.

TRUISMS

"No one is satisfied with his fortune nor dissatisfied with his intellect."

–Nicolas Boileau-Despreaux, <u>Satires</u> (II)

My affirmations:

_____
_____
_____
_____

What I am inquiring into:

_____
_____
_____
_____

My planned actions:

_____
_____
_____
_____

TRUISMS—CONTINUED

28) "An intention without action is like a fart in the wind."

Suggested Affirmation: "I appreciate the value of intentions as they are needed to set up the action phase."

Suggested Inquiry: Intention is the first phase of success. It is an ingredient and action is the mixing.

Suggested Action: Each time you affirm your intention, bring action along with it.

SUCCESS/DEFINITION/RESULTS

"Satisfaction lies in the effort, not in the attainment. Full effort is full victory."

–Nicolas Boileau-Despreaux, <u>Satires</u> (II)

My affirmations:

_____
_____
_____
_____

What I am inquiring into:

_____
_____
_____
_____

My planned actions:

_____
_____
_____
_____

SUCCESS/DEFINITION/RESULTS

1) *"The bigger the failures you are willing to accept, the greater the successes you can achieve."*

Suggested Affirmation: "I achieve more than most as I am willing to accept failures easily."

Suggested Inquiry: Success and failure are but two sides of the same coin.

Suggested Action: Take a bigger jump with a project and risk a big failure for the chance of a big success.

2) *"The higher your tolerance for failure, the greater your chances for success."*

Suggested Affirmation: "I increase my chances for success by increasing my tolerance for failure."

Suggested Inquiry: One of the best chances for success is through high-risk failures.

Suggested Action: Take a chance to succeed by attempting action on your goals and plans.

SUCCESS/DEFINITION/RESULTS

"Those who seek for much are left in want of much. Happy is he to whom God has given, with sparing hand, as much as is enough."

–Horace (Quintus Horatius Flaccus), <u>Carmina</u>
(bk. III, 16, 42)

My affirmations:

_____
_____
_____
_____

What I am inquiring into:

_____
_____
_____
_____

My planned actions:

_____
_____
_____
_____

SUCCESS/DEFINITION/RESULTS—CONTINUED

3)   *"Success is the blossom that started as a seed within and was*
      fed with action."

Suggested Affirmation: "I feed my seeds with action."

Suggested Inquiry: Often it is the seed within that brings forth growth, healing, and health.

Suggested Action: Take action by affirming success.

4)   *"The highest form of success is making the best of oneself."*
      –Og Mandino

Suggested Affirmation: "I am the best me there is."

Suggested Inquiry: We never stand still; we are either growing or going back.

Suggested Action: Read a book, listen to a lecture, or take a self-improvement course.

SUCCESS/DEFINITION/RESULTS

"If the crow had been satisfied to eat his prey in silence, he would have had more meat and less quarreling and envy."

–Horace (Quintus Horatius Flaccus),
Epistles (I, 17, 50)

My affirmations:

_____
_____
_____
_____

What I am inquiring into:

_____
_____
_____
_____

My planned actions:

_____
_____
_____
_____

SUCCESS/DEFINITION/RESULTS—CONTINUED

5) *"Most failed attempts bring one closer to achievement."*

Suggested Affirmation: "I do not believe in failures; I just believe in results."

Suggested Inquiry: If taking an action brings you one step closer to success, is not that action one that is fruitful?

Suggested Action: Go back to the last failure you had on three projects/goals and discover its contribution to success.

6) *"Use the law of averages and the odds to achieve success."*

Suggested Affirmation: "I use the law of averages and I play the odds to be successful."

Suggested Inquiry: Why are most people willing to bet against the odds?

Suggested Action: Wait until the odds are in your favor before playing.

SUCCESS/DEFINITION/RESULTS

"Now, that's enough."

> *–Horace (Quintus Horatius Flaccus),*
> *Epistles (I, 5, 12)*

My affirmations:

_____

_____

_____

_____

What I am inquiring into:

_____

_____

_____

_____

My planned actions:

_____

_____

_____

_____

SUCCESS/DEFINITION/RESULTS—CONTINUED

7)   *"Success ebbs and flows like the tide."*

Suggested Affirmation: "I take and enjoy the success when it comes and I work and wait until the tide flows my way."

Suggested Inquiry: Can one take advantage of the ebb and flow and use both to his advantage?

Suggested Action: Look at each project and determine what stage each is at. Then take action on the projects/goals that are flowing.

8)   *"Success—when you help me help you help me."*

Suggested Affirmation: "When I help others I am almost always helped."

Suggested Inquiry: You get something from serving when you do not serve to get something.

Suggested Action: Help someone to help you and make sure both profit.

SUCCESS/DEFINITION/RESULTS

"The fastidious are unfortunate: nothing can satisfy them."

–Jean de la Fontaine, <u>Fables</u> (II, 1)

My affirmations:

_____
_____
_____
_____

What I am inquiring into:

_____
_____
_____
_____

My planned actions:

_____
_____
_____
_____

SUCCESS/DEFINITION/RESULTS—CONTINUED

9) *"Success is heavenly when people help people help each other succeed."*

Suggested Affirmation: "Success is heavenly when it is achieved with the help of others."

Suggested Inquiry: Sooner or later you will fall off of success mountain if you continue alone.

Suggested Action: Help someone achieve his or her success.

10) *"Success is either bitter or sweet; depending on what you did to achieve it, you need motivation."*

Suggested Affirmation: "My success is sweet."

Suggested Inquiry: What makes success sweet is when success is fathered by many.

Suggested Action: Before taking action, test your planned move.

11) *"If you want to succeed you must learn to live with failure."*

Suggested Affirmation: "I not only live with failure, I am energized by it."

Suggested Inquiry: Having a high tolerance for little or no measurable progress is the sweetest way to success.

Suggested Action: Celebrate a failure with a dinner out.

175

SUCCESS/DEFINITION/RESULTS

"He is very foolish who aims at satisfying all the world and his father."

–Jean de la Fontaine, <u>Fables</u> (III, 1)

My affirmations:

_____
_____
_____
_____

What I am inquiring into:

_____
_____
_____
_____

My planned actions:

_____
_____
_____
_____

SUCCESS/DEFINITION/RESULTS–CONTINUED

12) "More wisdom is gained from failure than from success."

Suggested Affirmation: "I am gaining wisdom with each failed attempt."

Suggested Inquiry: Having a gain from a failure is a discipline one must learn and continue to practice.

Suggested Action: Write down the areas in your life in which you gained wisdom from failed events.

13) "Success comes when intention is followed up with consistent action."

Suggested Affirmation: "My intention is good and my commitment is even stronger."

Suggested Inquiry: Intention without action leads to the path of frustration.

Suggested Action: I follow up all my intentions with action.

14) "Success fulfills intention."

Suggested Affirmation: "I succeed with my intentions because I work on my intentions."

Suggested Inquiry: Intention and affirmations cannot stand on their own; they need each other.

Suggested Action: Fulfill an intention by taking action.

SUCCESS/DEFINITION/RESULTS

"Satisfying a few to please many is bad."

*–Johann Christoph Friedrich
von Schiller, Votivtafeln*

My affirmations:

_____
_____
_____
_____

What I am inquiring into:

_____
_____
_____
_____

My planned actions:

_____
_____
_____
_____

SUCCESS/DEFINITION/RESULTS–CONTINUED

15) "Success starts being realized when action replaces intention."

Suggested Affirmation: "Intention is first and action brings it to life."

Suggested Inquiry: It is intention that makes action unique and focused.

Suggested Action: Keep the intention and act on the intention.

16) "At times the price of failure is higher than the price of success." –Tuchy

Suggested Affirmation: "The price of failure keeps me moving on the path of success."

Suggested Inquiry: Often to live failure is not an option as it costs too much.

Suggested Action: Affirm success and take action to succeed.

SUCCESS/DEFINITION/RESULTS

"There is no satisfaction in any good without a companion."

–Seneca (Lucius Annaeus Seneca), <u>Epistoloe Ad Lucilium</u> (VI)

My affirmations:

_____

_____

_____

_____

What I am inquiring into:

_____

_____

_____

_____

My planned actions:

_____

_____

_____

_____

SUCCESS/DEFINITION/RESULTS—CONTINUED

*17) "In most cases the more significant the success, the more
failures one must endure to achieve it."*

Suggested Affirmation: "I endure failures on my path to success
as it is worth the effort."

Suggested Inquiry: The more significant the success the more
that must be overcome to achieve it.

Suggested Action: Restart a stalled goal.

18) "Success–talent isn't enough."

Suggested Affirmation: "I add perseverance, willingness,
and determination as my ingredients to be added to talent to
succeed."

Suggested Inquiry: Many, many talented people do not achieve
success.

Suggested Action: Take action and plan the next action; write it
down and schedule it to be done.

SUCCESS/DEFINITION/RESULTS

"He is well paid that is well satisfied,
And I delivering you am satisfied,
And therein do account myself well paid;
My mind was never yet more mercenary."

—William Shakespeare, <u>The Merchant of Venice</u>
(Portia at IV, i)

My affirmations:

_____
_____
_____
_____

What I am inquiring into:

_____
_____
_____
_____

My planned actions:

_____
_____
_____
_____

SUCCESS/DEFINITION/RESULTS—CONTINUED

19) "Be grateful for your problems as they make success worthwhile."

Suggested Affirmation: "I understand and accept problems as my path to success."

Suggested Inquiry: One's problem becomes another's opportunity.

Suggested Action: Take any problem you are now facing and write down the potential opportunities that the problem offers.

20) "We all have succeeded in birth, and will succeed in death; how we succeed in between is up to us."

Suggested Affirmation: "I am grateful for the opportunity to create my own success."

Suggested Inquiry: We are always succeeding.

Suggested Action: At the end of the day write down all your successes, starting with successfully making it through the day.

SUCCESS/DEFINITION/RESULTS

"As long as I have a want, I have a reason for living. Satisfaction is death."

–William Shakespeare, <u>The Merchant of Venice</u>
(Portia at IV, i)

My affirmations:

_____
_____
_____
_____

What I am inquiring into:

_____
_____
_____
_____

My planned actions:

_____
_____
_____
_____

SUCCESS/DEFINITION/RESULTS—CONTINUED

21) *"The least of us has succeeded thousands of times and succeeds at something everyday."*

Suggested Affirmation: "I am successful every day of my life."

Suggested Inquiry: Everyone you see is successful.

Suggested Action: Begin the day by acknowledging your success; at midday acknowledge it again and finally, before retiring.

22) *"All succeed at what they choose to do."*

Suggested Affirmation: "I choose to succeed at what I do today."

Suggested Inquiry: We manifest success or failure based on our thoughts and action.

Suggested Action: Choose to succeed at something you have not succeeded at and take action.

SUCCESS/DEFINITION/RESULTS

"Enough is as good as a feast."

–Joshua Sylvester, <u>Works</u>

My affirmations:

_____
_____
_____
_____

What I am inquiring into:

_____
_____
_____
_____

My planned actions:

_____
_____
_____
_____

SUCCESS/DEFINITION/RESULTS—CONTINUED

23) "Success isn't permanent and failure isn't fatal." –Dick Butkus

Suggested Affirmation: "I go from success to success and I use failure as stepping stones."

Suggested Inquiry: Failure is not permanent and is waiting to be transformed into success.

Suggested Action: Take action on a goal in which you must fail at today to get to success at a future date.

24) "Success is a choice."

Suggested Affirmation: "I choose success."

Suggested Inquiry: The great news is that we can choose success and we can define what success means to us.

Suggested Action: Define success for each of the goals you have, especially those that are subjective.

25) "Success is a conversation."

Suggested Affirmation: "I create success by my speaking."

Suggested Inquiry: Conversation and action create success.

Suggested Action: Speak about your success for each goal, then write it down for later review.

SUCCESS/DEFINITION/RESULTS

"Give me, indulgent gods! With mind serene, and guiltless heart, to range the sylvan scene; No splendid poverty, no smiling care, No well-bred hate, or servile grandeur, there."

—Edward Young, <u>Love of Fame</u> *(satire I, l. 235)*

My affirmations:

_____
_____
_____
_____

What I am inquiring into:

_____
_____
_____
_____

My planned actions:

_____
_____
_____
_____

SUCCESS/DEFINITION/RESULTS—CONTINUED

26) *"Success comes to those who work while they wait."*

Suggested Affirmation: "I work while I wait."

Suggested Inquiry: Working makes waiting easier.

Suggested Action: Review each goal and upon review if one has no current action, then work on a task to move you closer to success.

27) *"The degree of success one attains is in direct proportion to the degree one takes action."*

Suggested Affirmation: "I take vigorous action on each goal or project."

Suggested Inquiry: Any action that brings me closer to success is good action.

Suggested Action: Review the action you are taking on each goal, then determine if you need more, or need to revise, your action.

GOOD THINGS/RESULTS

"Laziness may appear attractive, but work gives satisfaction."

–Anne Frank

My affirmations:

_____

_____

_____

_____

What I am inquiring into:

_____

_____

_____

_____

My planned actions:

_____

_____

_____

_____

_____

GOOD THINGS/RESULTS

1) *"Good things come to those who work while they wait. Good things come to those who wait while they work. Good things come to those who work while others wait."*

Suggested Affirmation: "Good things come to me because I am willing to work for them."

Suggested Inquiry: Good things happen when one begins to work for them.

Suggested Action: Begin working on an area of your life in need of good things.

2) *"Succeeding at bad things is far worse than failing at good things."*

Suggested Affirmation: "I am a total failure doing anything that is bad."

Suggested Inquiry: Inaction is best when action will result in achieving something bad.

Suggested Action: Stop one act that hurts you or others today.

GOOD THINGS/RESULTS

"Satisfaction lies in the effort, not in the attainment. Full effort is full victory."

–Mahatma Gandhi

My affirmations:

_____

_____

_____

_____

What I am inquiring into:

_____

_____

_____

_____

My planned actions:

_____

_____

_____

_____

GOOD THINGS/RESULTS—CONTINUED

3)   *"You can't tell, but you can judge a book by its cover." –The*
     Wall Street Journal

Suggested Affirmation: "The book of my life matches its cover
and both strive for excellence."

Suggested Inquiry: Speaking is one's cover; action is one's book.

Suggested Action: Take someone famous you have judged, read
his or her biography, and have that shift how you judge him or
her.

4)   *"Look within for strength; look beyond for perspective."*

Suggested Affirmation: "My strength comes from the divine
within–all I need do is look and listen for it."

Suggested Inquiry: Seeing the divine in others gives me the
perspective of the breath of God.

Suggested Action: Take a goal in which you are having trouble
and find another that has achieved it; find out what that person
did and take the same action.

HAPPINESS

"To be able to look back upon one's past life with satisfaction is to live twice."

—*Lord Acton*

My affirmations:

_____

_____

_____

_____

What I am inquiring into:

_____

_____

_____

_____

My planned actions:

_____

_____

_____

_____

HAPPINESS

1) *"Happiness is when what you think, what you say, and what you do are in harmony." —Gandhi*

Suggested Affirmation: "What I think, say, and do are in harmony, and that brings me happiness."

Suggested Inquiry: Happiness is a decision that is backed by action.

Suggested Action: After you decide, then speak and act on being happy.

2) *"A key to successful living: enjoy life, as it is yours to do with as you please."*

Suggested Affirmation: "I enjoy life."

Suggested Inquiry: We create our own joy by our attitude and actions.

Suggested Action: Do what you love.

HAPPINESS

"He who is not satisfied with himself will grow; he who is not sure of his own correctness will learn many things."

–Chinese proverb

My affirmations:

_____
_____
_____
_____

What I am inquiring into:

_____
_____
_____
_____

My planned actions:

_____
_____
_____
_____

HAPPINESS—CONTINUED

3) *"The question is not whether you are a success or a failure but rather are you succeeding or failing at what you want to do."*

Suggested Affirmation: "I am successful at what I do because what I do is what I love."

Suggested Inquiry: Doing what one loves works because one's heart is involved.

Suggested Action: Review your goals from the perspective of wanting to do them.

4) *"Success is like life–it is only worthwhile when it is used to do good."*

Suggested Affirmation: "I work to succeed at worthwhile things."

Suggested Inquiry: Success is sweet when it moves one toward worthwhile things.

Suggested Action: Scrap goals or projects that are not worthwhile from your perspective.

CARL "TUCHY" PALMIERI

HAPPINESS

"Whether you find satisfaction in life depends not on your tale of years, but on your will."

—*Michel Eyquem de Montaigne*

My affirmations:

_____
_____
_____
_____

What I am inquiring into:

_____
_____
_____
_____

My planned actions:

_____
_____
_____
_____

HAPPINESS—CONTINUED

5)   *"It does no good to acquire money, to get the things it can buy,*
     if you lose as a result of it the things that money cannot buy."
     —Tuchy

Suggested Affirmation: "I value the things that I have that money
cannot buy."

Suggested Inquiry: One must be mindful of the balance between
what money can buy and what it cannot buy and then not
sacrifice what it cannot buy for what it can.

Suggested Action: Make a list of what you have that money
cannot buy, post it where you can see it everyday, and add to it as
often as possible.

6)   *"With many aspects of life, if you make it a habit of giving more*
     than you get, more often than not you will get more than you
     give."

Suggested Affirmation: "I find that if I work at giving more than
I get, I often get more than I give."

Suggested Inquiry: Giving without expecting anything in return
is one of life's most worthwhile gifts.

Suggested Action: Do or give something anonymously.

HAPPINESS

"What exactly is success? For me it is to be found not in applause, but in the satisfaction of feeling that one is realizing one's ideal."

—Anna Pavlova

My affirmations:

_____

_____

_____

_____

What I am inquiring into:

_____

_____

_____

_____

My planned actions:

_____

_____

_____

_____

HAPPINESS—CONTINUED

7) *"Doing more than what is expected of you on a consistent basis will yield unexpected rewards in the future."*

Suggested Affirmation: "I do more than what is expected of me and I know my reward will come here on earth or in heaven."

Suggested Inquiry: What a world it would be if we all did more than what was expected.

Suggested Action: Surprise someone by doing more than they expect.

WORK

"The sounder your argument, the more satisfaction you get out of it."

–Edgar Watson Howe

My affirmations:

_____

_____

_____

_____

What I am inquiring into:

_____

_____

_____

_____

My planned actions:

_____

_____

_____

_____

WORK

1) *"Work as if you will live forever, and live as if you will die today."*

Suggested Affirmation: "I work as if I am going to live forever. And I live as if I am going to die today."

Suggested Inquiry: Knowing that one can die today is a powerful and a pleasant way to spend today.

Suggested Action: Live well today and enjoy. Put in a good day's work.

2) *"Action moves intention to achievement."*

Suggested Affirmation: "My intentions are backed up with action."

Suggested Inquiry: Intention without action leads to disillusion; intention with action brings results.

Suggested Action: Add action to your intentions.

WORK

"There is a certain degree of satisfaction in having the courage to admit one's errors. It not only clears up the air of guilt and defensiveness, but often helps solve the problem created by the error."

–Dale Carnegie

My affirmations:

_____

_____

_____

_____

What I am inquiring into:

_____

_____

_____

_____

My planned actions:

_____

_____

_____

_____

WORK—CONTINUED

3) *"Intention is just a start and must be followed up with action."*

Suggested Affirmation: "I get clear on my intention before I take action."

Suggested Inquiry: Intention alone is a form of giving over responsibility for results.

Suggested Action: Review and update your intentions to ensure that you have not revised them.

4) *"Intention dies with inaction and completes with action."*

Suggested Affirmation: "I give my intentions life through action."

Suggested Inquiry: Holding onto intention for the sake of the intention has little value.

Suggested Action: Remove an intention in which no action has been taken in three months.

5) *"The best attitude is 'keep-at-it-tude.'"*

Suggested Affirmation: "I am persistent in my action."

Suggested Inquiry: Your attitude determines your altitude and keeping at it brings success.

Suggested Action: Reinforce your attitude with persistent action.

WORK

"I feel sorry for the person who can't get genuinely excited about his work. Not only will he never be satisfied, but he will never achieve anything worthwhile."

—Walter Chrysler

My affirmations:

_____

_____

_____

_____

What I am inquiring into:

_____

_____

_____

_____

My planned actions:

_____

_____

_____

_____

WORK—CONTINUED

6) *"If you rest on your laurels you will crush them."*

Suggested Affirmation: "When I achieve one of my goals I acknowledge it, appreciate it, and move on to another goal."

Suggested Inquiry: One can get stuck with a success as easily as one gets stuck in failure.

Suggested Action: Let your new actions speak for you, rather than your past success.

7) *"Better to wear out the soles of your shoe than the backside of your pants."*

Suggested Affirmation: "My pants last for years; my shoes are resoled every year."

Suggested Inquiry: The ideal mix is one in which there is a balancing of wear on both the shoes and on the backside of one's pants.

Suggested Action: Give a good day's work and rest to regenerate for tomorrow.

WORK

"If the firms that employ an increasing majority of the population are driven solely to satisfy the owner's greed at the expense of working conditions, of the stability of the community, and of the health of the environment, chances are that the quality of our lives will be worse than it is now."

—Mihaly Csikszentmihalyi

My affirmations:

_____

_____

_____

_____

What I am inquiring into:

_____

_____

_____

_____

My planned actions:

_____

_____

_____

_____

WORK—CONTINUED

8) *"Success comes to those who work while they wait."*

Suggested Affirmation: "I work while I wait for my ship to come in."

Suggested Inquiry: Working while one waits makes waiting easier.

Suggested Action: Take action on any goal you are waiting for.

9) *"Often it is not whether one can succeed or fail but rather, is one willing to succeed?"*

Suggested Affirmation: "I am willing to succeed."

Suggested Inquiry: Willingness and perseverance are two keys to success.

Suggested Action: Discover a goal in which you lack willingness and either let the goal go or commit to being willing to achieve it.

WORK

*"Many business leaders today view their jobs as entailing
responsibility for the welfare of the wider community. These
individuals do not define themselves as profit-making machines
whose only reason for existing is to satisfy escalating expectation
for immediate gain."*

—Mihaly Csikszentmihalyi

My affirmations:

_____

_____

_____

_____

What I am inquiring into:

_____

_____

_____

_____

My planned actions:

_____

_____

_____

_____

WORK—CONTINUED

10) *"The degree of success one attains is in direct proportion to the degree one takes action."*

Suggested Affirmation: "I take action the moment it is called for."

Suggested Inquiry: Action leads to more action.

Suggested Action: Improve the degree of success on a project by taking more action.

11) *"Some people work hard at failing because of their fear of succeeding."*

Suggested Affirmation: "I am not afraid to fail or to succeed."

Suggested Inquiry: Fear of failing and fear of succeeding are but two sides of the same coin.

Suggested Action: Feel the fear and do it anyway.

WORK

"I am against religion because it teaches us to be satisfied with not understanding the world."

—Richard Dawkins

My affirmations:

_____

_____

_____

_____

What I am inquiring into:

_____

_____

_____

_____

My planned actions:

_____

_____

_____

_____

WORK—CONTINUED

12) *"The hardest job one can do is nothing, because you do not know when you are finished."*

Suggested Affirmation: "I always know if I am finished or not."

Suggested Inquiry: It is easier to know when you are complete by the action or lack of action that you take.

Suggested Action: Take a job in which you are doing nothing, do something, and discover that you know better when you are in action.

13) *"The dictionary is the only place you will find 'success' before 'work.'"*

Suggested Affirmation: "In my dictionary, 'work' comes before 'success.'"

Suggested Inquiry: Work makes success sweeter when achieved.

Suggested Action: Work towards success on a lingering project.

WORK

"When clouds form in the skies we know that rain will follow but we must not wait for it. Nothing will be achieved by attempting to interfere with the future before the time is ripe. Patience is needed."

–I Ching

My affirmations:

_____

_____

_____

_____

What I am inquiring into:

_____

_____

_____

_____

My planned actions:

_____

_____

_____

_____

WORK—CONTINUED

14) "'Success' is found in the dictionary between 'determination' and 'work.'"

Suggested Affirmation: "I use work and determination as my keys to success."

Suggested Inquiry: Determination and work are the twin brothers of success.

Suggested Action: While working, affirm your determination to succeed/complete.

15) "An intention without action is like a fart in the wind."

Suggested Affirmation: "I combine action with my intention to have my kite fly in the wind."

Suggested Inquiry: Action is the kite that allows the wind of intention to be useful.

Suggested Action: Bring action to each intention and bring intention to each action.

WORK

"The individual investor should act consistently as an investor and not as a speculator. This means that he should be able to justify every purchase he makes and each price he pays by impersonal, objective reasoning that satisfies him that he is getting more than his money's worth for his purchase."

–Benjamin Graham

My affirmations:

_____

_____

_____

_____

What I am inquiring into:

_____

_____

_____

_____

My planned actions:

_____

_____

_____

_____

WORK—CONTINUED

16) *"There is no achievement without action."*

Suggested Affirmation: "I achieve because I am a man of action."

Suggested Inquiry: All success comes from one determined action or inaction.

Suggested Action: Review your goals and find one that to achieve the result you want requires no action on your part.

17) *"Early to bed, early to rise, makes a man healthy, wealthy and wise."*

Suggested Affirmation: "I rise early and I go to bed early to achieve life's benefits."

Suggested Inquiry: Giving up early on one side diminishes one's power; giving up early on both sides is disaster waiting.

Suggested Action: Go to bed early for one week and rise early.

18) *"None of the secrets of success will work unless you do."*

Suggested Affirmation: "My foundational secret to success is my wiliness to work."

Suggested Inquiry: Is work the real secret to success, or is it just one key?

Suggested Action: Add work to each goal that you have.

CHANGE

"I have found no greater satisfaction than achieving success through honest dealing and strict adherence to the view that, for you to gain, those you deal with should gain as well."

–Alan Greenspan

My affirmations:

_____

_____

_____

_____

What I am inquiring into:

_____

_____

_____

_____

My planned actions:

_____

_____

_____

_____

CHANGE

1) *"Change is constant, and the truth changes."*

Suggested Affirmation: "I know the truth changes."

Suggested Inquiry: The truth changes through conversation, through time, and through many other unknown factors.

Suggested Action: Change the truth through action; i.e., do something you have never done before.

2) *"If change is constantly occurring, then the truth is constantly changing."*

Suggested Affirmation: "The truth is always changing."

Suggested Inquiry: Not all truths change at the same time and in the same interval, but truths do indeed change.

Suggested Action: Change the truth through your action.

CHANGE

"Now we've got around seven thousand people working, and that to me is fantastically satisfying, more than dollars and cents, because I just believe that the greatest thing you can give someone is a job."

–Janet Holmes a Court

My affirmations:

_____

_____

_____

_____

What I am inquiring into:

_____

_____

_____

_____

My planned actions:

_____

_____

_____

_____

CHANGE—CONTINUED

3) *"Our problem is that we live as if truth is constant, when in reality change is constant and because of that, truth changes."*

Suggested Affirmation: "I live my life knowing that change is constant and that at one time or another, the truth changes."

Suggested Inquiry: When we really look we see that change is occurring all around us.

Suggested Action: Keep the truth from changing by staying consistent with a commitment.

4) *"Change makes havoc with truth, because with the law of change, impossible becomes possible."*

Suggested Affirmation: "By changing and altering my action I make the impossible possible."

Suggested Inquiry: The law of change is a law that is never broken, even when it appears to have been broken.

Suggested Action: Make something possible in your life through change.

CHANGE

"The faster we grew, the more stores we had open, the more money we made. Employees move quickly up the ranks of a company that's growing fast. Shareholders made a lot of money. If you invested $25,000 from January 1987 to January 1994, you'd have more than a million dollars. I get a lot of personal satisfaction from that."

—Wayne Huizenga

My affirmations:

_____
_____
_____
_____

What I am inquiring into:

_____
_____
_____
_____

My planned actions:

_____
_____
_____
_____

CHANGE—CONTINUED

5)   "Change makes impossible, impossible."

Suggested Affirmation: "The law of change makes 'impossible' a word found only in the dictionary of fools."

Suggested Inquiry: Every man can make impossible impossible by using the law of change.

Suggested Action: Make "impossible" impossible in some way.

6)   "Most people find that the comforts of life are actually not that comfortable."

Suggested Affirmation: "I appreciate my comforts in life."

Suggested Inquiry: Some comforts are more comfortable than others.

Suggested Action: Give up any comfort in life that is not comfortable.

GOD

"Don't just work for the money–that will bring only limited satisfaction."

–Kathy Ireland

My affirmations:

_____

_____

_____

_____

What I am inquiring into:

_____

_____

_____

_____

My planned actions:

_____

_____

_____

_____

GOD

1) "With God, 'impossible' is impossible."

Suggested Affirmation: "With God all things are possible."

Suggested Inquiry: God can do all things and with God we can do all things.

Suggested Action: Turn over a difficult task to God and be willing to do the footwork when he tells you.

2) "The hand of God comes gloved in the hands of ordinary people."

Suggested Affirmation: "God works through man."

Suggested Inquiry: The hand of God can be seen in people, places, and things.

Suggested Action: Be the hand of God today.

GOD

"If I regarded my life from the point of view of the pessimist, I should be undone. I should seek in vain for the light that does not visit my eyes and the music that does not ring in my ears. I should beg night and day and never be satisfied. I should sit apart in awful solitude, a prey to fear and despair. But since I consider it a duty to myself and to others to be happy, I escape a misery worse than any physical deprivation."

–Helen Keller

My affirmations:

_____

_____

_____

_____

What I am inquiring into:

_____

_____

_____

_____

My planned actions:

_____

_____

_____

_____

GOD—CONTINUED

3)   "Failure is your teacher, sent from God."

Suggested Affirmation: "I take failed attempts as lessons sent from God to help me on my journey."

Suggested Inquiry: God is always on your side and rooting for you. He will never give you anything you cannot handle.

Suggested Action: Learn the lesson from your teacher.

4)   "The kingdom of heaven is within." –Jesus

Suggested Affirmation: "I know that a spark of the divine lies within me and when I am in the presence of that divine I am indeed in heaven."

Suggested Inquiry: Jesus promised us heaven on earth. Sometimes we cannot see the kingdom.

Suggested Action: Nurture the kingdom within through prayer, meditation, and quiet time.

GOD

"Under private property, each tries to establish over the other an alien power, so as thereby to find satisfaction of his own selfish need. The increase in the quantity of objects is therefore accompanied by an extension of the realm of the alien powers to which man is subjected, and every new product represents a new potentiality of mutual swindling and mutual plundering."

–Karl Marx

My affirmations:

_____
_____
_____
_____

What I am inquiring into:

_____
_____
_____
_____

My planned actions:

_____
_____
_____
_____

GOD—CONTINUED

5)   *"Prayer without action is no prayer at all."*

Suggested Affirmation: "When I pray I am in action as I stay present to my prayer."

Suggested Inquiry: The power of prayer grows as one devotes time and energy to it.

Suggested Action: Start with prayers of thanks and gratitude and finish with prayers for the world.

6)   *"Meditation is the key to success."*

Suggested Affirmation: "Through meditation I hear the word of God and that is the successful word."

Suggested Inquiry: Many types of meditation with one purpose– to get to the divine.

Suggested Action: Learn to meditate.

SUCCESS SECRETS

"When I hear bad news I look at it as another leadership test that will determine how successful Go Daddy will become. So I no longer dread it. Instead, I enjoy the game of finding the very best way to deal with it, and take great satisfaction in having a hand in resolving the issues that come my way."

—Bob Parsons

My affirmations:

_____

_____

_____

_____

What I am inquiring into:

_____

_____

_____

_____

My planned actions:

_____

_____

_____

_____

SUCCESS SECRETS

1)   "It's up to you."

Suggested Affirmation: "My success is up to me."

Suggested Inquiry: Success is helped or hurt by one's beliefs, actions, attitudes, and persistence.

Suggested Action: Keep the responsibility and delegate the action to increase the manifestation of your goal.

2)   "Do what successful people do."

Suggested Affirmation: "I do what successful people do."

Suggested Inquiry: Modeling a successful person is the surest and safest path to success.

Suggested Action: Find the person who has what you want and do what that person did.

3)   "If you persist long enough you eventually succeed."

Suggested Affirmation: "I keep going until I succeed."

Suggested Inquiry: Persisting and showing up together account for ninety-nine percent of success.

Suggested Action: Be persistent on all things that matter to you.

SUCCESS SECRETS

"The really happy people are those who have broken the chains of procrastination, those who find satisfaction in doing the job at hand. They're full of eagerness, zest, productivity. You can be, too."

–Norman Vincent Peale

My affirmations:

_____

_____

_____

_____

What I am inquiring into:

_____

_____

_____

_____

My planned actions:

_____

_____

_____

_____

SUCCESS SECRETS—CONTINUED

4) *"A secret is knowing that giving up is the ultimate tragedy."*

Suggested Affirmation: "I know that giving up is the ultimate tragedy, so I do not give up."

Suggested Inquiry: Failure cannot and will not exist unless one gives up.

Suggested Action: Get up; never give up.

5) *"Work, work, work."*

Suggested Affirmation: "Three of the most powerful words to achieve success are work, work, work."

Suggested Inquiry: Nothing works without work of one kind or another.

Suggested Action: Enjoy working on your goals and projects.

6) *"Go the extra mile." –Jesus*

Suggested Affirmation: "Going the extra mile produces miracles."

Suggested Inquiry: Success often is just around the corner.

Suggested Action: Take one more action.

233

SUCCESS SECRETS

"As long as I have a want, I have a reason for living. Satisfaction is death."

–George Bernard Shaw

My affirmations:

_____

_____

_____

_____

What I am inquiring into:

_____

_____

_____

_____

My planned actions:

_____

_____

_____

_____

SUCCESS SECRETS—CONTINUED

7)   "Take profit from loss."

Suggested Affirmation: "I take profit from loss by looking for and getting the lesson from each failed attempt."

Suggested Inquiry: The only true loss is when you do not get something good from it.

Suggested Action: Take the time to journalize the gain from the day's losses and successes.

8)   "Failures repeated differently bring one closer to the successful attempt."

Suggested Affirmation: "I make sure that I improve with each attempt and revise it to bring me closer to the final and successful attempt."

Suggested Inquiry: Finding ways that do not work brings one closer to finding ways that do work.

Suggested Action: Review your last attempt for three goals and discover what needs to be changed to improve on the attempt.

SUCCESS SECRETS

"Laziness may appear attractive, but work gives satisfaction."

–Anne Frank

My affirmations:

_____

_____

_____

_____

What I am inquiring into:

_____

_____

_____

_____

My planned actions:

_____

_____

_____

_____

SUCCESS SECRETS—CONTINUED

9)   "Turning 'want' power into willpower."

Suggested Affirmation: "I turn 'want' power into willpower by being in action."

Suggested Inquiry: Willpower and the ability to take action increases one's level of success in all areas.

Suggested Action: Take an area in which you have want power (wish power) and turn it into willpower by action.

10) "Make failure your teacher."

Suggested Affirmation: "I make failure my teacher by taking profit from a loss."

Suggested Inquiry: Failure often is your most important teacher.

Suggested Action: Help another find their teacher.

11) "Having a high naturally."

Suggested Affirmation: "I get a natural high when I am in action."

Suggested Inquiry: One can derive a great deal of satisfaction through action, even when the results of the action are disappointing.

Suggested Action: Get high on action.

SUCCESS SECRETS

"He who possesses the source of enthusiasm will achieve great things. Doubt not. You will gather friends around you as a hair clasp gathers the hair."

—I Ching

My affirmations:

_____
_____
_____
_____

What I am inquiring into:

_____
_____
_____
_____

My planned actions:

_____
_____
_____
_____

SUCCESS SECRETS—CONTINUED

12) "You are about as successful as you make up your mind to be."

Suggested Affirmation: "I am very successful."

Suggested Inquiry: You are the ultimate judge of your degree of success.

Suggested Action: Write down all the areas in your life where you are successful.

13) "Many actions that at first view look like failures, actually are but stepping stones to a bigger success."

Suggested Affirmation: "I do not believe in failure; I believe in results."

Suggested Inquiry: With all action you succeed in producing a result, so from that vantage point it is a success.

Suggested Action: Acknowledge all the stepping stones you have walked on through action.

SUCCESS SECRETS

"To be able to look back upon one's past life with satisfaction is to live twice."

–Lord Acton

My affirmations:

_____

_____

_____

_____

What I am inquiring into:

_____

_____

_____

_____

My planned actions:

_____

_____

_____

_____

SUCCESS SECRETS—CONTINUED

14) *"When one succeeds that is good; when all succeed, that is miraculous."*

Suggested Affirmation: "Life is miraculous as we are all succeeding."

Suggested Inquiry: All that we see is, to one degree or another, success.

Suggested Action: Help another succeed and create a miracle.

15) *"To succeed by helping others to succeed is the most fulfilling success of all."*

Suggested Affirmation: "My success is sweet as I help others succeed."

Suggested Inquiry: Time and time again, program after program, and divine messages have validated the fact that real success comes from helping others to succeed.

Suggested Action: Help another succeed.

SUCCESS SECRETS

"He who is not satisfied with himself will grow; he who is not sure of his own correctness will learn many things."

–Chinese proverb

My affirmations:

_____
_____
_____
_____

What I am inquiring into:

_____
_____
_____
_____

My planned actions:

_____
_____
_____
_____
_____

SUCCESS SECRETS—CONTINUED

16) "Opportunities knock, but success must be pursued."

Suggested Affirmation: "I pursue my opportunities."

Suggested Inquiry: Pursuing opportunity increases one's chance for success exponentially.

Suggested Action: Look at an opportunity and decide to pursue it.

17) "The secrets to success are well known."

Suggested Affirmation: "I know the secrets to success."

Suggested Inquiry: What must I do to employ the secrets of success that I already know?

Suggested Action: Write down all the secrets of success that you already know.

18) "Success is often just an idea away."

Suggested Affirmation: "I look forward to a new idea."

Suggested Inquiry: Meditating on and thinking about how to achieve goals are great ways to have new ideas come to one.

Suggested Action: Go over a goal and write down possible ways to achieve that goal.

SUCCESS SECRETS

"Whether you find satisfaction in life depends not on your tale of years, but on your will."

—Michel Eyquem de Montaigne

My affirmations:

_____

_____

_____

_____

What I am inquiring into:

_____

_____

_____

_____

My planned actions:

_____

_____

_____

_____

SUCCESS SECRETS—CONTINUED

19) "Success is, an amazing amount of time, a positive manipulation of failure."

Suggested Affirmation: "I manipulate failure in a positive way as a method of achieving success."

Suggested Inquiry: How can one positively manipulate failure?

Suggested Action: Manipulate failure by taking profit from the loss.

20) "Success often comes to those who are too busy to look for it."

Suggested Affirmation: "I pursue my goals and success comes when I am not looking."

Suggested Inquiry: It is when we are busy working and doing that the angel of success appears.

Suggested Action: Be busy.

SUCCESS SECRETS

"What exactly is success? For me it is to be found not in applause, but in the satisfaction of feeling that one is realizing one's ideal."

—*Anna Pavlova*

My affirmations:

_____

_____

_____

_____

What I am inquiring into:

_____

_____

_____

_____

My planned actions:

_____

_____

_____

_____

SUCCESS SECRETS—CONTINUED

21) *"A little daily dose of success is enough to keep most of us going."*

Suggested Affirmation: "All I need is a daily dose of success."

Suggested Inquiry: What is the dosage you need to keep going?

Suggested Action: Acknowledge your dosage of success by stating, "I have taken action."

22) *"Success often comes from not knowing your limitations."*

Suggested Affirmation: "For me, limitation does not exist."

Suggested Inquiry: The only way one knows their limitations is to go beyond them.

Suggested Action: Do something you know is beyond your capability.

23) *"Today's success was yesterday's failure that would not give up."*

Suggested Affirmation: "I never give up."

Suggested Inquiry: Giving up is the ultimate tragedy.

Suggested Action: Try again.

SUCCESS SECRETS

"The sounder your argument, the more satisfaction you get out of it."

−Edgar Watson Howe

My affirmations:

_____

_____

_____

_____

What I am inquiring into:

_____

_____

_____

_____

My planned actions:

_____

_____

_____

_____

SUCCESS SECRETS—CONTINUED

24) "Failures repeated differently are the secret to success."

Suggested Affirmation: "I never make the same mistake twice."

Suggested Inquiry: An altered attempt is one's way of honoring one's commitment.

Suggested Action: Purposely alter attempt made.

25) "A secret to success is to enjoy the failures along the way."

Suggested Affirmation: "I enjoy the failures along the way."

Suggested Inquiry: We are in failure more often than in success.

Suggested Action: Enjoy each and every attempt and laugh whenever you can.

PROBLEMS

"Show me a thoroughly satisfied man and I will show you a failure."

—*Thomas Alva Edison (1847-1931)*

My affirmations:

_____

_____

_____

_____

What I am inquiring into:

_____

_____

_____

_____

My planned actions:

_____

_____

_____

_____

PROBLEMS

1) *"The only time your life will be without problems is when it's over."*

Suggested Affirmation: "I gratefully accept problems as a part of this wonderful life."

Suggested Inquiry: Your thinking can resolve problems and can create them.

Suggested Action: Change one problem into an opportunity by your speaking.

2) *"Man's purpose in life is to overcome problems until the problems overcome him."*

Suggested Affirmation: "Problems overcome me when I am laid to rest, and when that happens all my problems disappear."

Suggested Inquiry: The more problems one solves in life the less are carried to the grave with him.

Suggested Action: Accept a problem that is truly yours and leave the rest.

PROBLEMS

"He is a wise man who does not grieve for the things which he has not, but rejoices for those which he has."

–Epictetus (50-120)

My affirmations:

_____

_____

_____

_____

What I am inquiring into:

_____

_____

_____

_____

My planned actions:

_____

_____

_____

_____

PROBLEMS—CONTINUED

3)   *"As with most things in life, if you resist problems, your
      problems will persist."*

Suggested Affirmation: "I acknowledge, allow, and tackle my
problems."

Suggested Inquiry: Acknowledging a problem is the most
important step to solving it.

Suggested Action: Take a goal that has no action going on and
locate, then acknowledge, it.

4)   *"The problem is that many of us are looking in the wrong book
      to find the secrets to success."*

Suggested Affirmation: "I look in the book of wisdom to find my
success."

Suggested Inquiry: The book of wisdom has been penned by
many.

Suggested Action: Read and study this book on success.

PROBLEMS

"He is rich that is satisfied."

–Thomas Fuller (1608-1661)

My affirmations:

_____

_____

_____

_____

What I am inquiring into:

_____

_____

_____

_____

My planned actions:

_____

_____

_____

_____

PROBLEMS—CONTINUED

5) *"A problem is a problem is a problem when you say it is a problem."*

Suggested Affirmation: "I believe all problems have the seed of opportunity within them."

Suggested Inquiry: Our speaking turns problems into problems, and our speaking turns them into opportunities.

Suggested Action: Take what you have been calling a problem and make it an opportunity to turn it into an opportunity.

6) *"Be grateful for your problems as they make your successful employment happen."*

Suggested Affirmation: "I am grateful for my problems."

Suggested Inquiry: Problems are only problems when you say they are problems.

Suggested Action: Thank God for your problems today and see how they are helping you.

THOUGHTS TO PONDER

"Looking at small advantages prevents great affairs from being accomplished."

—*Confucius*

My affirmations:

_____
_____
_____
_____

What I am inquiring into:

_____
_____
_____
_____

My planned actions:

_____
_____
_____
_____

THOUGHTS TO PONDER

1) *"Thinking is the determining factor in the realm of possibility and impossibility."*

Suggested Affirmation: "In terms of possibility and impossibility, my thinking is that all things are possible with God."

Suggested Inquiry: If it's possible for another human being, it is possible for you.

Suggested Action: Think positively about each goal and pray over them.

2) *"A cup of knowledge, a barrel of love, and an ocean of sweat lead to success."*

Suggested Affirmation: "I bring my sweat equity into the pursuit of my goals."

Suggested Inquiry: Check into the amount of sweat you are willing to put into a project or goal before you commit to it.

Suggested Action: Double the amount of sweat you are putting in a project that has stalled.

THOUGHTS TO PONDER

"Whether you find satisfaction in life depends not on your tale of years, but on your will."

–Michel Eyquem de Montaigne

My affirmations:

_____
_____
_____
_____

What I am inquiring into:

_____
_____
_____
_____

My planned actions:

_____
_____
_____
_____

THOUGHTS TO PONDER—CONTINUED

3)   *"Commitment is the glue that binds goals and aspirations to achievement."*

Suggested Affirmation: "Before I write a goal I make a commitment to my commitment."

Suggested Inquiry: Goals and aspirations are just goals and aspiration, without commitment.

Suggested Action: Review your goals and test them against your commitment. Let go of goals that are not aligned with your commitment.

4)   *"The strongest memory is weaker than the palest ink."*
     –Chinese proverb

Suggested Affirmation: "I enhance my memory by putting to pen the important items that I want to remember correctly."

Suggested Inquiry: One's memory gets mixed up over time unless reinforced with the written word.

Suggested Action: Journal the important events of the day to remember.

THOUGHTS TO PONDER

"Satisfaction consists in freedom from pain, which is the positive element of life."

−*Arthur Schopenhauer (1788-1860)*

My affirmations:

_____

_____

_____

_____

What I am inquiring into:

_____

_____

_____

_____

My planned actions:

_____

_____

_____

_____

THOUGHTS TO PONDER—CONTINUED

5) *"Opportunities taken create new opportunities."*

Suggested Affirmation: "I take advantage of as many opportunities as I can because I know they will lead to new opportunities."

Suggested Inquiry: Do opportunities create new opportunities?

Suggested Action: Take advantage of an opportunity today and plan for the new opportunity it created.

6) *"Winning is habit-forming."*

Suggested Affirmation: "I am in the habit of winning–I love it and appreciate it."

Suggested Inquiry: Both winning and losing are habit-forming.

Suggested Action: If you are in the habit of losing, then set a goal and develop a plan to win.

THOUGHTS TO PONDER

"To be able to look back upon one's past life with satisfaction is to live twice."

—*Lord Acton (1834-1902)*

My affirmations:

_____

_____

_____

_____

What I am inquiring into:

_____

_____

_____

_____

My planned actions:

_____

_____

_____

_____

THOUGHTS TO PONDER—CONTINUED

7)   "Success is sometimes doing the wrong thing wrong."

Suggested Affirmation: "I am willing to accept success from doing the wrong thing wrong."

Suggested Inquiry: Success can come from doing the wrong thing wrong and can come from doing the right thing wrong.

Suggested Action: Look at a failed attempt from two perspectives: what was the outcome and what does that achieve? What was the outcome and what can you learn from it?

8)   "Many of life's greatest achievements have nothing to do with success or failure, but rather are a result of failing at what one was trying to achieve (the discovery of rubber)."

Suggested Affirmation: "I am open to have success come as a result of a failure in another area."

Suggested Inquiry: Research the accidental achievements and use them to motivate you to keep action going.

Suggested Action: Take every failure and look at it from the view of unintended consequences.

THOUGHTS TO PONDER

"I am easily satisfied with the very best."

–Winston Churchill (1874-1965)

My affirmations:

_____
_____
_____
_____

What I am inquiring into:

_____
_____
_____
_____

My planned actions:

_____
_____
_____
_____

THOUGHTS TO PONDER—CONTINUED

9) *"Often one's success is unknown to others until their eulogy is given."*

Suggested Affirmation: "I promote my success when needed and keep it private when appropriate."

Suggested Inquiry: Waiting for one's eulogy may not be the best route to continued success.

Suggested Action: Promote any success that requires promotion to create a new and bigger success.

10) *"One's success can be one's failure."*

Suggested Affirmation: "I know that what is success for me today can be viewed by another as a failure."

Suggested Inquiry: Successes are successes and failures are failures by virtue of judgment.

Suggested Action: Take a stand that failures do not exist except in our speaking

THOUGHTS TO PONDER

*"Look at a day when you are supremely satisfied at the end.
It's not a day when you lounge around doing nothing; it's when
you've had everything to do, and you've done it."*

−*Margaret Thatcher*

My affirmations:

_____
_____
_____
_____

What I am inquiring into:

_____
_____
_____
_____

My planned actions:

_____
_____
_____
_____

THOUGHTS TO PONDER—CONTINUED

11) "A successful act viewed by one may be viewed as a failure by another."

Suggested Affirmation: "I measure success by my standards rather than by the standards of others."

Suggested Inquiry: Only the participant truly knows if success has been achieved, as success is more often than not a perspective.

Suggested Action: Take a previous view where you declared a failure and view it from the perspective that it was a success.

12) "Going with the flow often takes one down the wrong place."

Suggested Affirmation: "Before I go with the flow I check to make sure the flow is going in the direction I want to go."

Suggested Inquiry: Going with the flow can be either good or bad.

Suggested Action: Go with the flow today, where appropriate.

THOUGHTS TO PONDER

"Man always assumed that he was more intelligent than dolphins because he had achieved so much–the wheel, New York, wars, and so on–while all the dolphins had ever done was muck about in the water having a good time. But conversely, the dolphins had always believed that they were far more intelligent than man–for precisely the same reason."

–Douglas Noel Adams

My affirmations:

_____
_____
_____
_____

What I am inquiring into:

_____
_____
_____
_____

My planned actions:

_____
_____
_____
_____

THOUGHTS TO PONDER—CONTINUED

13) *"The wise man takes profit from a loss; the fool takes a loss from profit."*

Suggested Affirmation: "I take profit from the loss."

Suggested Inquiry: Success can be turned into failure by taking loss from it.

Suggested Action: Find the profit in every action today, whether successful or not.

14) *"The bigger the success, the bigger the failure before it."*

Suggested Affirmation: "I accept today's big failure for tomorrow's bigger success."

Suggested Inquiry: Accepting failure as part of success makes success possible.

Suggested Action: Look back at your last success and discover the previous failures that led to it.

CARL "TUCHY" PALMIERI

THOUGHTS TO PONDER

*"You can have anything you want–if you want it badly enough.
You can be anything you want to be, do anything you set out
to accomplish, if you hold to that desire with singleness of
purpose."*

–William Adams

My affirmations:

_____
_____
_____
_____

What I am inquiring into:

_____
_____
_____
_____

My planned actions:

_____
_____
_____
_____

THOUGHTS TO PONDER—CONTINUED

15) *"One reason most people do not succeed at greatness is that they are unwilling to have great failures."*

Suggested Affirmation: "I am willing to have great failures so that I can experience great success."

Suggested Inquiry: Great failures often are as important as great successes.

Suggested Action: Take a big chance; bigger than you have ever done.

16) *"Success, like life, is but a journey."*

Suggested Affirmation: "I journey through life being successful."

Suggested Inquiry: Making success part of your journey makes the journey worthwhile.

Suggested Action: Plan for success by writing your plan for it on your journey through time.

271

THOUGHTS TO PONDER

"Good writers define reality; bad ones merely restate it. A good writer turns fact into truth; a bad writer will, more often than not, accomplish the opposite."

—*Edward Albee*

My affirmations:

_____

_____

_____

_____

What I am inquiring into:

_____

_____

_____

_____

My planned actions:

_____

_____

_____

_____

THOUGHTS TO PONDER—CONTINUED

17) "You are ruled by everything until you understand the power of doing nothing." –Two Bunch Palms Resort and Spa

Suggested Affirmation: "I understand the power of doing nothing."

Suggested Inquiry: We are always doing something; the act of doing nothing is something.

Suggested Action: Go to a spa and do nothing.

18) "Some men spend their lives doing nothing and other men spend their lives not ever doing nothing."

Suggested Affirmation: "I spend my life on doing things that will outlast it."

Suggested Inquiry: Being and doing are not the same, and yet, at times, both are called for.

Suggested Action: Before doing, check in with your intuitive side to see if it is the right action.

THOUGHTS TO PONDER

"Optimism is essential to achievement and it is also the foundation of courage and true progress."

–Lloyd Alexander

My affirmations:

_____
_____
_____
_____

What I am inquiring into:

_____
_____
_____
_____

My planned actions:

_____
_____
_____
_____

THOUGHTS TO PONDER—CONTINUED

19) *"There are times in life when doing nothing is the most important thing you can do."*

Suggested Affirmation: "I stand back when it's appropriate."

Suggested Inquiry: Doing nothing can be the most difficult task, even when you know it is the right thing to do.

Suggested Action: Resist making a move when it is clear that a move is not the right action.

20) *"Men who work at nothing find it easy to play at everything, and men who work at everything find it hard to do nothing at play."*

Suggested Affirmation: "I balance work and play."

Suggested Inquiry: Balancing is the most effective way to live life.

Suggested Action: When working, work; when playing, play; and do each every day.

THOUGHTS TO PONDER

"People of mediocre ability sometimes achieve outstanding success because they don't know when to quit. Most men succeed because they are determined to."

–George Herbert Allen

My affirmations:

_____

_____

_____

_____

What I am inquiring into:

_____

_____

_____

_____

My planned actions:

_____

_____

_____

_____

THOUGHTS TO PONDER—CONTINUED

21) *"Though no one can go back and make a brand new start, anyone can start from now and make a brand new ending."*
   –Anonymous

Suggested Affirmation: "Today is a new day."

Suggested Inquiry: Starting again allows for a new beginning.

Suggested Action: Make a brand new start on an old ending.

WHAT IS SUCCESS?

"I don't want to achieve immortality through my work. I want to achieve it through not dying."

–Woody Allen

My affirmations:

_____
_____
_____
_____

What I am inquiring into:

_____
_____
_____
_____

My planned actions:

_____
_____
_____
_____

WHAT IS SUCCESS?

1) *"When all parties win."*

Suggested Affirmation: "I believe in win/win."

Suggested Inquiry: The most rewarding wins are when all participants win.

Suggested Action: Come from win/win with all your transactions today.

2) *"Accidental success–when you succeed at something by accident."*

Suggested Affirmation: "I am grateful for any accidental successes I am given."

Suggested Inquiry: Being open to accidental successes allows them to occur.

Suggested Action: When pursuing a goal and you find that it is taking a slightly different direction, look and see if shifting may be that accidental success.

WHAT IS SUCCESS?

"There is no such thing as can't; only won't. If you're qualified, all it takes is a burning desire to accomplish, to make a change. Go forward, go backward. Whatever it takes! But you can't blame other people or society in general. It all comes from your mind. When we do the impossible we realize we are special people."

–Jan Ashford

My affirmations:

_____

_____

_____

_____

What I am inquiring into:

_____

_____

_____

_____

My planned actions:

_____

_____

_____

_____

WHAT IS SUCCESS?—CONTINUED

3) *"The least of us are amongst the most successful of all creation."*

Suggested Affirmation: "I know that every last one of us is so successful, as we were born initially, and have negotiated through many aspects of life."

Suggested Inquiry: Making it through the day requires hundreds of little successes.

Suggested Action: Take the time one morning to write down what one has to complete successfully in just one aspect of life, such as getting up and getting to work.

4) *"Well-paid is being well-earned."*

Suggested Affirmation: "I am well paid and I earn my pay."

Suggested Inquiry: Payment takes many forms and earning is often not immediate.

Suggested Action: Increase your pay by taking other earnings from your work.

WHAT IS SUCCESS?

"The humorous man recognizes that absolute purity, absolute justice, absolute logic and perfection are beyond human achievement and that men have been able to live happily for thousands of years in a state of genial frailty."

–(Justin) Brooks Atkinson

My affirmations:

_____
_____
_____
_____

What I am inquiring into:

_____
_____
_____
_____

My planned actions:

_____
_____
_____
_____

WHAT IS SUCCESS?—CONTINUED

*5)   "Let the sweet taste of success overpower the bitterness of
      failure."*

Suggested Affirmation: "I enjoy the sweet taste of success while
on the path through my imagination."

Suggested Inquiry: Imagining the sweet taste of success does
indeed counter the bitterness of failed attempts.

Suggested Action: Acknowledge when a failure occurred, be
grateful, and take from that failure the successful elements.

*6)   "If you take stumbling blocks and put one on top of the other
      they will become the stairs to success; if not, they remain
      tripping stones."*

Suggested Affirmation: "I put my stumbling blocks to good use
by placing one on top of the other."

Suggested Inquiry: A tripping stone for one is a building block
for another as one picked it up.

Suggested Action: Turn each stumble into a pathway to success
by learning from it.

WHAT IS SUCCESS?

"Nothing whatever pertaining to godliness and real holiness can be accomplished without grace."

–Saint Augustine

My affirmations:

_____

_____

_____

_____

What I am inquiring into:

_____

_____

_____

_____

My planned actions:

_____

_____

_____

_____

WHAT IS SUCCESS?—CONTINUED

7) *"You can only fail if you have a specific result to be achieved."*

Suggested Affirmation: "I succeed and fail because I have specific actions to be achieved."

Suggested Inquiry: To succeed at nothing is the biggest failure of all.

Suggested Action: Take any goal that is not specific and make it specific.

8) *"The wise man has learned to turn 'want' power into willpower."*

Suggested Affirmation: "I turn my 'want' power into willpower through action." ·

Suggested Inquiry: Willpower must be backed up with action to have success.

Suggested Action: Turn your "want" power to willpower through affirmations, visualizations, and actions.

WHAT IS SUCCESS?

"When you're young, the silliest notions seem the greatest achievements."

–Pearl Bailey

My affirmations:

_____

_____

_____

_____

What I am inquiring into:

_____

_____

_____

_____

My planned actions:

_____

_____

_____

_____

WHAT IS SUCCESS?—CONTINUED

9)   *"The only fatal mistake is the one in which you learn absolutely nothing."*

Suggested Affirmation: "I learn something from every mistake."

Suggested Inquiry: Take profit from your mistakes.

Suggested Action: At the end of the day record what you have learned.

10)   *"Many of the world's most successful people fail more often than many of life's failures."*

Suggested Affirmation: "I fail a lot and I succeed a lot."

Suggested Inquiry: The more you fail the more you succeed.

Suggested Action: Increase the number of attempts by one hundred percent.

OTHER SUCCESS SAYINGS

"Nothing splendid has ever been achieved except by those who dared believe that something inside of them was superior to circumstance."

–Bruce Barton

My affirmations:

_____

_____

_____

_____

What I am inquiring into:

_____

_____

_____

_____

My planned actions:

_____

_____

_____

_____

OTHER SUCCESS SAYINGS

1)   "Often spontaneity gets credit when one has failed to plan."

Suggested Affirmation: "I plan my day and I allow for spontaneity when circumstances call for it."

Suggested Inquiry: Using spontaneity as an excuse for not planning often is the lazy way out.

Suggested Action: Make a plan in an area of your life that is not going as well as you would like.

2)   "Some men achieve success by working hard; some men achieve success by working smart, and still others achieve it by working hard and smart."

Suggested Affirmation: "I work hard and I work smart."

Suggested Inquiry: Sometimes one must work hard and smart to achieve the result needed.

Suggested Action: Balance your goals by working smarter on those your gut tells you and work harder on those you know you are not working hard enough on.

OTHER SUCCESS SAYINGS

"Age is only a number; a cipher for the records. A man can't retire his experience. He must use it. Experience achieves more with less energy and time."

—Bernard Mannes Baruch

My affirmations:

_____
_____
_____
_____

What I am inquiring into:

_____
_____
_____
_____

My planned actions:

_____
_____
_____
_____

OTHER SUCCESS SAYINGS—CONTINUED

3) *"Success comes when you take universal laws and make them personal."*

Suggested Affirmation: "I accept and work with the universal laws."

Suggested Inquiry: Universal laws that are personalized are one's greatest assets.

Suggested Action: Listen to Brian Tracey's audio on Universal Laws.

4) *"Success and money have nothing in common."*

Suggested Affirmation: "I gauge my success in terms other than money."

Suggested Inquiry: While money can be used as a barometer of success, real success goes well beyond it.

Suggested Action: Take time today to discover what success means to you without considering money as an ingredient.

OTHER SUCCESS SAYINGS

"Having once decided to achieve a certain task, achieve it at all costs of tedium and distaste. The gain in self-confidence of having accomplished a tiresome labor is immense."

–Thomas Arnold Bennett

My affirmations:

_____
_____
_____
_____

What I am inquiring into:

_____
_____
_____
_____

My planned actions:

_____
_____
_____
_____

OTHER SUCCESS SAYINGS—CONTINUED

5) *"Making a decision is a good step; acting on it is success."*

Suggested Affirmation: "I act quickly once I decide to do something."

Suggested Inquiry: In many cases, the mere act is itself success.

Suggested Action: Once you make a decision to do something, take action on it as soon as practical.

6) *"Be grateful for your failures as they make success a possibility."*

Suggested Affirmation: "I am grateful for each attempt I make as they make success a possibility."

Suggested Inquiry: The greater the number of thought-out attempts, the greater the possibility of success.

Suggested Action: Add failed attempts to your gratitude list.

7) *"The path to success is paved with the bricks of persistence and perseverance."*

Suggested Affirmation: "I am persistent and I persevere."

Suggested Inquiry: Trying again and again and giving it all you have each attempt are key ingredients.

Suggested Action: Double the number of attempts you make on achieving a specific goal and with each attempt hang in longer.

OTHER SUCCESS SAYINGS

"The elementary school must assume as its sublime and most solemn responsibility the task of teaching every child in it to read. Any school that does not accomplish this has failed."

–William John Bennett

My affirmations:

_____

_____

_____

_____

What I am inquiring into:

_____

_____

_____

_____

My planned actions:

_____

_____

_____

_____

OTHER SUCCESS SAYINGS—CONTINUED

8)   *"Opening the mind is a start, quieting the internal voices is progress, and having an open heart is success."*

Suggested Affirmation: "I keep an open mind, I quiet my internal voices, and have an open heart."

Suggested Inquiry: Being open includes one's mind, heart, and ears.

Suggested Action: Create a goal of improving your openness by five hundred percent.

9)   *"The gates of success swing on the hinges of action and persistence."*

Suggested Affirmation: "I am a man of action and I am persistent."

Suggested Inquiry: Action that is altered after each failed attempt is a form of persistence.

Suggested Action: Develop the art of persistence by going one more step.

OTHER SUCCESS SAYINGS

"Great things are accomplished by talented people who believe they will accomplish them."

—Warren G. Bennis

My affirmations:

_____

_____

_____

_____

What I am inquiring into:

_____

_____

_____

_____

My planned actions:

_____

_____

_____

_____

OTHER SUCCESS SAYINGS—CONTINUED

10) "Success stands on the foundation of failure. Failure stands on the foundation of failure."

Suggested Affirmation: "I continue to build my foundation through successive and thought-out failures."

Suggested Inquiry: Often the foundations are the same; the failure just stopped building.

Suggested Action: Keep building the foundation by making successive attempts.

11) "In failure there is success. In foolishness there is wisdom."

Suggested Affirmation: "I know the paradox of success and wisdom–both come from having been a failure and a fool."

Suggested Inquiry: What leads to wisdom and success?

Suggested Action: Learn from your failure and your foolishness.

12) "In every success there are many failures."

Suggested Affirmation: "Wisdom tells me that many failures may be required to achieve success."

Suggested Inquiry: More often than not success comes after many failures.

Suggested Action: Make a game out of failures by using them as a rising barometer.

297

OTHER SUCCESS SAYINGS

"You cannot believe in honor until you have achieved it. Better keep yourself clean and bright: you are the window through which you must see the world."

–*Sir Walter Besant*

My affirmations:

_____
_____
_____
_____

What I am inquiring into:

_____
_____
_____
_____

My planned actions:

_____
_____
_____
_____

OTHER SUCCESS SAYINGS—CONTINUED

13) "A successful person fails until he succeeds, and a failure succeeds until he fails."

Suggested Affirmation: "I count each failure as a stepping stone that is bringing me closer to my success."

Suggested Inquiry: Failure turns into success; the only mystery is when.

Suggested Action: Press on and make another attempt today.

14) "The path of success and the path of failure are often the same; the only difference is one's willingness to continue."

Suggested Affirmation: "I continue on my path until I reach my goal."

Suggested Inquiry: Stopping is the only way failure can occur.

Suggested Action: Start up a goal or project in which there is no activity and/or you abandoned.

15) "Be grateful for failures as they make success possible."

Suggested Affirmation: "I am grateful for my failures as they make my success possible."

Suggested Inquiry: An attitude of gratitude increases your altitude.

Suggested Action: This evening make a gratitude list for the opportunity to fail.

OTHER SUCCESS SAYINGS

"If we fight a war and win it with H-bombs, what history will remember is not the ideals we were fighting for but the methods we used to accomplish them. These methods will be compared to the warfare of Genghis Khan, who ruthlessly killed every last inhabitant of Persia."

–Hans Albrecht Bethe

My affirmations:

_____
_____
_____
_____

What I am inquiring into:

_____
_____
_____
_____

My planned actions:

_____
_____
_____
_____

OTHER SUCCESS SAYINGS—CONTINUED

16) "The bridge of success is actually built upon the foundation of failure."

Suggested Affirmation: "I built my bridge to success on as many foundational bricks of failure as I need."

Suggested Inquiry: A paradox of life–that success is built on the foundation of failure.

Suggested Action: Build your bridges through tasks.

17) "The success of your internal marriage determines the success of your external marriage."

Suggested Affirmation: "I attend to my internal marriage by attending to it spiritually, emotionally, and spiritually."

Suggested Inquiry: Integrity and wholeness are internal commitments made in the bond of internal marriage.

Suggested Action: Read a book; take a course on dealing with the internal you.

18) "Failure is just the first step on the pathway of success."

Suggested Affirmation: "I go for success and I know that often the first step to success is a failed attempt."

Suggested Inquiry: A 747 jet on auto-pilot is not on course ninety-five percent of the time and yet it succeeds in getting to its destination.

Suggested Action: Take corrective action after each failed attempt.

OTHER SUCCESS SAYINGS

"About the most originality that any writer can hope to achieve honestly is to steal with good judgment."

–Josh Billings

My affirmations:

_____
_____
_____
_____

What I am inquiring into:

_____
_____
_____
_____

My planned actions:

_____
_____
_____
_____

OTHER SUCCESS SAYINGS—CONTINUED

19) "The successful person allows himself to fail."

Suggested Affirmation: "I allow myself to fail many times on my way to success."

Suggested Inquiry: The more one fails, the more one succeeds.

Suggested Action: Go and allow yourself to fail every day.

20) "Success comes from failing a different way until you fail to fail."

Suggested Affirmation: "My key to success is I never fail the same way twice."

Suggested Inquiry: Failing a different way is a form of success.

Suggested Action: Make three attempts and if success is not achieved, alter the attempt and try again and again.

21) "It is the little people who are big enough to make you successful."

Suggested Affirmation: "I do not allow my past success to make me too big for my britches."

Suggested Inquiry: Often it is the past success who becomes too big to hold on and allows the smaller person to become bigger than they are.

Suggested Action: Find a success in your life in which you are resting on your laurels and commit to be small and humble enough to get bigger and better with it.

OTHER SUCCESS SAYINGS

"What looks like a loss may be the very event which is subsequently responsible for helping to produce the major achievement of your life."

–Srully D. Blotnick

My affirmations:

_____

_____

_____

_____

What I am inquiring into:

_____

_____

_____

_____

My planned actions:

_____

_____

_____

_____

OTHER SUCCESS SAYINGS—CONTINUED

22) "People who are successful do things they don't like to do."
   –Cynde Denson

Suggested Affirmation: "I am willing to do the things I do not like to do to achieve the success that I am reaching for."

Suggested Inquiry: It is often in doing what one does not like to do that leads one to get what one wants.

Suggested Action: Do that task that you have been avoiding that is between you and success.

23) "Eighty percent of success is showing up."

Suggested Affirmation: "I show up and take action."

Suggested Inquiry: Deciding to start on a project or goal is eighty percent of one's success.

Suggested Action: Show up on a new project or goal today through action.

24) "Success is a public affair. Failure is a private matter."

Suggested Affirmation: "I do not shout about my success and do not hide my failures."

Suggested Inquiry: Using one's energy hiding failures leaves that much less to pursue success.

Suggested Action: Let your successes speak for themselves and share your failed attempts with others.

OTHER SUCCESS SAYINGS

"Studies indicate that the one quality all successful people have is persistence. They're willing to spend more time accomplishing a task and to persevere in the face of many difficult odds. There's a very positive relationship between people's ability to accomplish any task and the time they're willing to spend on it."

–Dr. Joyce Brothers

My affirmations:

_____
_____
_____
_____

What I am inquiring into:

_____
_____
_____
_____

My planned actions:

_____
_____
_____
_____

OTHER SUCCESS SAYINGS—CONTINUED

*25) "Probably the biggest advantage of success is that you don't
have to listen to good advice."*

Suggested Affirmation: "I will always listen to advice and
afterwards determine if I am to put it aside or follow it."

Suggested Inquiry: Taking advice from one that has failed in
your attempt can be very valuable in your pursuit.

Suggested Action: Seek the advice of those who traveled the path
before you so that you do not make the same mistakes.

26) "Behind every successful man is a surprised mother-in law."

Suggested Affirmation: "I pleasantly surprise people with my success."

Suggested Inquiry: Surprising people with your success is also a
gift to them as it often encourages them to move towards success.

Suggested Action: Surprise your loved ones today with success.

*27) "Coming together is a beginning; keeping together is progress,
and working together is success."*

Suggested Affirmation: "I work easily and effortlessly with all
people on the project."

Suggested Inquiry. Surrounding oneself with the best people is
the surest path to success.

Suggested Action: Commit to work with a teammate or replace
that teammate.

OTHER SUCCESS SAYINGS

"The way to develop self-confidence is to do the thing you fear and get a record of successful experiences behind you. Destiny is not a matter of chance, it is a matter of choice; it is not a thing to be waited for, it is a thing to be achieved."

—William Jennings Bryan

My affirmations:

_____
_____
_____
_____

What I am inquiring into:

_____
_____
_____
_____

My planned actions:

_____
_____
_____
_____

OTHER SUCCESS SAYINGS—CONTINUED

28) "Success—if you have tried something and failed you are vastly better off than if you tried to do nothing and succeeded."

Suggested Affirmation: "I am grateful for the attempts I made in all aspects of my life whether I succeeded or not as I am better off for it."

Suggested Inquiry: Attempting something new is a success in its own right.

Suggested Action: Attempt something new.

29) "You must experience failure to appreciate success."

Suggested Affirmation: "I use my failed experiences as stepping stones to success."

Suggested Inquiry: The more effort one puts into achieving success the more fulfilling it becomes.

Suggested Action: Take action on your most difficult project and acknowledge that action after it is complete; then visualize success with it.

30) "The road to success is always under construction."

Suggested Affirmation: "I realize that success is a building project."

Suggested Inquiry: Continually building on success is the surest way to creating satisfying success.

Suggested Action: Take a successful project and duplicate it for another project.

OTHER SUCCESS SAYINGS

"I don't wait for moods. You accomplish nothing if you do that. Your mind must know it has got to get down to work."

—Pearl S. Buck

My affirmations:

_____

_____

_____

_____

What I am inquiring into:

_____

_____

_____

_____

My planned actions:

_____

_____

_____

_____

OTHER SUCCESS SAYINGS—CONTINUED

31) "Failure is a part of success."

Suggested Affirmation: "I truly believe failure is a vital part of success."

Suggested Inquiry: The more you fail the more you succeed.

Suggested Action: Go fail today in a way that brings you closer to success.

32) "The degree of success is directly proportional to the degree of risk."

Suggested Affirmation: "I take the appropriate and bold risks to achieve success."

Suggested Inquiry: The biggest risk of all is to risk nothing.

Suggested Action: Take a project in which you have stopped because you do not want to risk failing, and list what is the worst that can happen. Decide to either take the risk or remove the project from your goal list.

33) "Failure is the source of success." —Joe Palmer

Suggested Affirmation: "I use each failure to bring me closer to success."

Suggested Inquiry: Take profit from success.

Suggested Action: Review a recent attempt, make a revision you believe will work, and attempt it once more.

OTHER SUCCESS SAYINGS

"The young do not know enough to be prudent, and therefore they attempt the impossible, and achieve it, generation after generation."

—Pearl S. Buck

My affirmations:

_____
_____
_____
_____

What I am inquiring into:

_____
_____
_____
_____

My planned actions:

_____
_____
_____
_____

OTHER SUCCESS SAYINGS—CONTINUED

34) "The door of success swings on the hinges of obstacles."

Suggested Affirmation: "I know that obstacles are but bumps in the road that I must go over to achieve success."

Suggested Inquiry: Obstacles are what make success sweeter when achieved.

Suggested Action: Remove the obstacle through altered attempts and thoughtful action.

35) "Failure teaches success."

Suggested Affirmation: "I use past failure as my teacher."

Suggested Inquiry: Using past failure as one's teacher is the way to profit from a loss.

Suggested Action: Just before taking action, ask yourself how this action differs from the previous action that failed.

36) "Success is a decision we make."

Suggested Affirmation: "I decide that I will succeed."

Suggested Inquiry: We must decide to succeed before we can succeed.

Suggested Action: Make a decision to succeed in an area that you have not succeeded at but are committed to succeed at.

OTHER SUCCESS SAYINGS

"Nothing stops the man who desires to achieve. Every obstacle is simply a course to develop his achievement muscle. It's a strengthening of his powers of accomplishment."

–Eric Butterworth

My affirmations:

_____

_____

_____

_____

What I am inquiring into:

_____

_____

_____

_____

My planned actions:

_____

_____

_____

_____

OTHER SUCCESS SAYINGS—CONTINUED

37) "Organization is the key to success."

Suggested Affirmation: "I keep myself organized knowing that to do so is my clearest path to success."

Suggested Inquiry: The level of one's organization is often based on personal comfort.

Suggested Action: Bring organization to an area of your life in which you see disorganization hindering you.

38) "Success is fathered by many; failure is an orphan."

Suggested Affirmation: "I have many fathers and I am never alone."

Suggested Inquiry: When working one's goals and projects, asking for God's help keeps one from feeling like an orphan during the times of failed attempts and gives one the strength to get up again.

Suggested Action: Take your most difficult goal and ask God for help each day and before each attempted action.

OTHER SUCCESS SAYINGS

"Most of the important things in the world have been accomplished by people who have kept on trying when there seemed to be no help at all."

–Dale Carnegie

My affirmations:

_____
_____
_____
_____

What I am inquiring into:

_____
_____
_____
_____

My planned actions:

_____
_____
_____
_____

OTHER SUCCESS SAYINGS—CONTINUED

*39) "One worthwhile task carried to a successful conclusion is
worth half a hundred unfinished tasks."*

Suggested Affirmation: "I complete my tasks in the proper
order."

Suggested Inquiry: Completing a task brings new energy that
helps one to complete another task.

Suggested Action: Complete one task and pat yourself on the
back for it.

40) "Disorganization is a key to success."

Suggested Affirmation: "I am organized in my disorganization."

Suggested Inquiry: Two dangers in life are order and disorder.

Suggested Action: Create the level of order and disorder in your
life that is your clearest route to success.

OTHER SUCCESS SAYINGS

*"If you make a habit of sincere prayer, your life will be very
noticeably and profoundly altered. Prayer stamps with its indelible
mark our actions and demeanor. A tranquility of bearing, a facial
and bodily repose, are observed in those whose inner lives are
thus enriched. Properly understood, prayer is a mature activity
indispensable to the fullest development of personality. Only in prayer
do we achieve that complete and harmonious assembly of body, mind,
and spirit which gives the frail human reed its unshakable strengths."*

–Alexis Carrel

My affirmations:

_____

_____

_____

_____

What I am inquiring into:

_____

_____

_____

_____

My planned actions:

_____

_____

_____

_____

OTHER SUCCESS SAYINGS—CONTINUED

41) "A true friend is one who overlooks your failures and tolerates your success." –Anonymous

Suggested Affirmation: "I am a true friend and I look for true friends."

Suggested Inquiry: A friend helps you to succeed and when you do, rejoices in it; and when you fail, that friend consoles and encourages you.

Suggested Action: Console and encourage a friend.

42) "You are a success to the degree that you feel warm and loving towards yourself."

Suggested Affirmation: "I am the judge of my success and I judge myself successful."

Suggested Inquiry: What one considers a success another may not deem so.

Suggested Action: Write down and acknowledge all the areas in your life that you are currently successful at. Start with your birth. (You succeeded at being born.)

319

OTHER SUCCESS SAYINGS

"If you fear making anyone mad, then you ultimately probe for the lowest common denominator of human achievement. If you wait for the perfect moment when all is safe and assured, it may never arrive. Mountains will not be climbed, races won, or lasting happiness achieved."

–Maurice Chevalier

My affirmations:

_____

_____

_____

_____

What I am inquiring into:

_____

_____

_____

_____

My planned actions:

_____

_____

_____

_____

OTHER SUCCESS SAYINGS—CONTINUED

43) "A 12-step program paradox: Where giving up is success."

Suggested Affirmation: "Admitting that one cannot do it alone and asking for help is a path to success."

Suggested Inquiry: Surrendering to God and asking for His help is always available to us and in some cases may be the only path to success.

Suggested Action: Ask God for help on a problem you cannot solve alone.

44) "The first requisite of success is the ability to apply your physical and mental energies to one problem without becoming weary."

Suggested Affirmation: "I give my problems my physical and mental energy until I succeed."

Suggested Inquiry: One can get energized by tackling a problem one considers worthwhile.

Suggested Action: The next time you work on a problem, affirm that it is what you want to be solved; see yourself solving it, then put your physical and mental energy into it.

CARL "TUCHY" PALMIERI

OTHER SUCCESS SAYINGS

"Of all the inventions that have helped to unify China perhaps the airplane is the most outstanding. Its ability to annihilate distance has been in direct proportion to its achievements in assisting to annihilate suspicion and misunderstanding among provincial officials far removed from one another or from the officials at the seat of government."

–Madame Chiang

My affirmations:

_____
_____
_____
_____

What I am inquiring into:

_____
_____
_____
_____

My planned actions:

_____
_____
_____
_____

OTHER SUCCESS SAYINGS—CONTINUED

45) "'Impossible' is a word found only in the dictionary of fools."

Suggested Affirmation: "My dictionary does not have the word 'impossible' in it."

Suggested Inquiry: To know what's impossible one must go beyond it.

Suggested Action: List the things you once though were impossible and you now find are possible.

46) "Making a decision is a good start; acting on it is success."

Suggested Affirmation: "Once I make a decision, I take action on it as soon as appropriate."

Suggested Inquiry: A decision without action is really not a decision.

Suggested Action: Take any decision you have made in which no current action is being taken, make a decision to act, then act.

ALSO BY CARL "TUCHY" PALMIERI:

The Platinum Rule and Other Contrarian Sayings
(BookSurge, 2006)

Tuchy's Law and Other Contrarian Quotes to Help You In Life's
Journey
(BookSurge, 2007)

Off The Wall Contrarian Quotes For People In Recovery
(BookSurge, 2007)

The Food Contrarian: Quotes for People Recovering From or
Dealing With Eating Issues
(BookSurge, 2007)

The Godsons
(BookSurge, 2007)

Josephine, In Her Words: Our Mom
(BookSurge, 2007)

Phil, In His Words: Our Dad
(BookSurge, 2007)

ALSO BY CARL "TUCHY" PALMIERI:

Relationship Magic
(BookSurge, 2008)

Money And So Much More: The True Meaning of Wealth
(BookSurge, 2008)

Sex and Intimacy: The Gifts of Life
(BookSurge, 2008)

When Man Listens: Everyone Can Listen to God
by Cecil Rose, reprinted by Carl "Tuchy" Palmieri
(BookSurge, 2008)

Relationship Recovery
(BookSurge, 2008)

Oprah, In Her Words: Our American Princess
(BookSurge, 2008)

The Conversion of the Church
by Sam Shoemaker, reprinted by Carl "Tuchy" Palmieri
(BookSurge, 2008)

ABOUT THE AUTHOR

Carl "Tuchy" Palmieri was born in 1942 in an old mansion belonging to the former mill owner of the factory where his father worked. His family was one of six related families that occupied the mansion. The second son of Italian immigrants, Carl grew up in Westport, Connecticut. After receiving a bachelor's degree in business administration from the University of Bridgeport he began his career marketing and installing accounting computers for the Burroughs Corporation. Twenty-one years later, in 1987, he started his own computer business. Carl is also the author of a series of self-help books.

Today Carl lives with his wife, Susan, in Fairfield, Connecticut. He has three children, two stepchildren, and 12 grandchildren. His nickname, Tuchy, comes from having been one of three Carls in his family. There was a "Big Carl," a "Carl the Twin," and "Carluch," which meant "Little Carl." "Carluch" evolved into "Carlatuch," "Tuch," and finally, "Tuchy."